My Journey
To Divine Healing

My Journey
To Divine Healing

HEALING THE WAY JESUS DID IT—
Salvation* Healing* Authority

HENRY E. DORSEY

Teacher / Pastor

authorHOUSE®

AuthorHouse™
1663 Liberty Drive
Bloomington, IN 47403
www.authorhouse.com
Phone: 1-800-839-8640

First published by AuthorHouse   05/24/2011

ISBN: 978-1-4634-1284-5 (sc)
ISBN: 978-1-4634-1673-7 (ebk)

Library of Congress Control Number: 2011908574

Printed in the United States of America

Any people depicted in stock imagery provided by Thinkstock are models, and such images are being used for illustrative purposes only.
Certain stock imagery © Thinkstock.

This book is printed on acid-free paper.

Because of the dynamic nature of the Internet, any web addresses or links contained in this book may have changed since publication and may no longer be valid. The views expressed in this work are solely those of the author and do not necessarily reflect the views of the publisher, and the publisher hereby disclaims any responsibility for them.

CONTENTS

My Journey To Divine Healing

What did Jesus do for us when he was crucified and died on a cross. In this book you will not only discover what Jesus did when he died for us, you will understand why. Your Christian heritage and covenant will be restored to you

The work of this undertaking is to strengthen The 'Followers of Jesus'. To equip and prepare The Saints for the 'Hands-on work of Healing and Deliverance and Freedom from the bondage of sickness, illness and disease. Too bring them to the Knowledge that JESUS IS THE SAME YESTERDAY, TODAY AND FOREVER. (Hebrew 8:13)

Henry E. Dorsey

11/24/2010

PERFACE

This book is written for the benefit of the Body of Jesus Christ, called to be Saints according to the scripture. It is my firm conviction that the body of Christ is fully capable of doing the work that Jesus has called us to do in the great commission.

This book is dedicated to the teaching and implementation of the 'How To' and 'How Does It Work 'elements of the Bible, described as the Kingdom of God.

It is my intent to provide a hands-on, practical approach to what the Bible says and not depend on recent customs or historical church traditions say about healing. I will also endeavor to give my perspective on the current movement of the Holy Spirit in the Church of Christ, and show current conditions of the typical struggling Church, as it pertains to restraining the Holy Spirits' work. I will confirm the Holy Spirit as comforter, who teaches us all things and leads us into all Righteousness.

I will establish a foundation for my Journey to Divine Healing' through my life experiences, struggles, bad teaching, misconceptions, faulty thinking and outright misunderstanding. As a result of my story, I hope your foundations in Jesus are strengthened and expanded.

It is my sincere hope that whoever reads this book, will be touched in a responsive place in their heart and spur them into God's work full force with the confidence that only the truth can reveal.

I dedicate this book to Cheryl and Janet my first and second born who have encouraged and inspired me to undertake this labor of love. In addition, my grandsons David and Jeremy are living proof of the provisions taught in this book. I bless them and put favor over their lives.

A special thanks to Ed Harris who diligently taped for me each week the lessons put to print in this book, as we studied the word of God together in their home for three (3) years. We witnessed many healings and deliverances by the power of the Holy Spirit and the Angelic Hosts.

INTRODUCTION

As I undertook to put to print the many experiences and events that bring this book to life, I had to consider in detail, what I would include and what I would exclude. The choice was difficult but was made with logic and Biblical reasoning. So, for this reason, I will examine the vital elements of the Bible which lend light to the view that Divine Healing is alive and well in our day and in our time.

Also, the major religious themes in contemporary Christianity will be dissected and examined in light of what the Bible actually says. Denominational issues will also be examined and discussed.

Most religious people want to believe in their religion of whatever the brand. Their main issues appear to be, does my religion meet my needs, and can I trust the leaders. Very seldom do religious people question their denomination or their leaders on substantive issues. This allows for long-standing Church traditions and practices to go unexamined and un-checked. There are times however, which do require the Christian Church to re-examine its practices and customs, especially in light of events, such as Israel becoming a Nation in one day (May 14[th]1948), which altered the way the Church and the new Jewish Nation would see each other and pursue their perceived roles in the world. I also refer to the concept of Replacement Theology, (which I will discuss later).

It is my hope that this book will assist someone along their journey in divine healing and inform them enough to pass it along to others. It is my firm conviction that, God knew what He was doing when He gave gifts unto men when He sent the Holy Spirit to in-dwell mankind on the day of Pentecost. I am also fully persuaded that The Holy Spirit has gifted me to teach and make His Word clear to the Body of Jesus Christ through the Healing gifts to His Church. In addition to the teaching gift, I have been granted the gift of of healings which I exercise in order to demonstrate that the Word of God is true and the power of God is real.

CHAPTER 1

ORIGINS

In all things pertaining to man-kind, questions arise. Where did we come from? Where are we going? Who started all of this? How do we fit into this creation or did we evolve by some unknown process. What—ever our response we make decisions based on information, good or bad, substantial or flimsy, logical or emotional. Whatever the case, we base our behavior on what we know or think we know. Generally, the proof of our belief system is 'Results'. Therefore, what—ever is stated as truth will be tested and validated by those who are of a mind to engage the truth.

Pontius Pilot asked Jesus 'What is Truth'? Jesus did not reply. Prior to the question asked by Pontius Pilot of Jesus, Jesus, during his ministry, made a statement to his disciples, 'You shall know the truth and the truth shall make you free'. The difference is, on the one hand, Pilot is making a statement about his own lack of knowledge of truth, and on the other hand Jesus, is giving a blue print to his disciples as to the effect of truth after knowing the truth, Truth will SET YOU FREE. (John 8:32)

What shall we be set free from? That is the major question. Shall we be free from ourselves, from sin, from sickness, from our nature, from our unregenerate life, from death, or, from the unseen world. We must go back to the the statement that Jesus made to the disciples, 'The Truth', which says, that there is a singular Truth which we must be aware of is real and that this singular truth stands alone and has an ability to SET US FREE from anything that encumbers us. This would include anything that comes against our mind, our health, our body or our spirit.

As with me and you, we had to learn many of God's Principles by hit and miss, but often missing the point, as we all have done. However during the past 15 years I have taken to heart (mind) the very words of Jesus and put them into practice. The results have been outstanding and not open to debate because I am an eye witness of these things. This is my testimony.

JOURNEY TO DIVINE HEALING

As with any journey, it began with the first step. My first step was taking the Bible and reading it as truth and an account from God of our origins, written by the hand of man but given to man by the Spirit of God.(1 Corinthians 2:4-16)

(v4) 'And my speech and my preaching was not with enticing words of man's wisdom, but in demonstration of the Spirit and of power: That your faith should not stand in the wisdom of men, but the power of God . . . . (v9) . . . . But as it is written, Eye hath not seen, nor ear heard, neither have entered into the heart of man, the things which God hath prepared for them that love him. But God hath revealed them to us by his Spirit; for the Spirit searches all things, yes, the deep things of God. For what man knows the things of a man, save the spirit of man which is in him? Even so, the things of God, knows no man but by the Spirit of God. Now we have received, not the spirit of the world, but the Spirit which is of God; that we might know the things that are freely given to us of God. Which things also we speak, not in words which man's wisdom teaches, but which the Holy Ghost (Spirit) teaches; comparing spiritual things with spiritual. But the natural man receives not the things of the Spirit of God; for they are foolishness unto him; neither can he know them, because they are spiritually discerned. But he that is spiritual judges all things, yet he himself is not judged of any man. For who has known the mind of the Lord, that he may instruct him? But we have the mind of Christ'.

Having understood the passage written by Paul the apostle, which establishes our authority under the Holy Spirit and not the spirit of man, my journey to divine healing was assured. All that was needed now was to know how I have had the mind of Christ and the way the Holy Spirit teaches us the mysteries of God.

I have read the Bible from cover to cover a few times. I did not really understand or see the picture God was painting with just the **knowledge of the word.** For me, I had to know what His **purpose** was in giving us the information. So I began to re-read the Bible with new eyes. The Holy Spirit impressed me with a verse that I have read many times, '**I will hear your prayers**' So, I prayed out loud for God to show me what I should see in His Word so that I could see His Purpose in His Word. Insight came almost immediately.

GENESIS

The book of beginnings gives the complete blue print of how God set up his Kingdom and how He ordered His creation. God spoke everything into being. This revelation has been the leading principle that has guided my journey to divine healing. Now the blue-print of the spoken word maybe applied to all of the provisions God gives to **man-kind for healing and all other activities under man-kinds authority. This provision applies to both Men and Women.** (Genesis 1:26)

(Genesis1:26) 'And God said, Let us make man in our image, after our likeness; and let them have dominion (Authority) over the fish of the sea, and over the fowl of the air, and over the cattle, and over all the earth and every creeping thing that creeps upon the earth.'

In addition, (Genesis 5:1-2) states;

(Genesis 5:1-2) This is the book of the generations of **ADAM. In the day that God made man**, in the **likeness** of God made he him; (v2) **Male and female created he them,** and blessed them, and **called THEIR name ADAM,** in the day they were created.

The pattern of authority and provision are established at the very beginning in the word of God. This pattern is seen in the **word of God** given to **Adam** when He gave him instruction concerning the **Tree of the Knowledge of good and evil. From this time forward GOD always gave man verbal instruction thru Himself or the Prophets, and the Angels.**

After the fall of **Adam,** thru disobedience, God had to re-order the creation in-order to redeem back what **Adam gave away to Lucifer (**the devil). The flood was the way God had determined to bring man-kind back to his original created dominion, untainted by angel DNA. God had to do it through an untainted **man. That man was Jesus of Nazareth, born in Bethlehem. Jesus, 'son of man' which is the title name Jesus gave himself spoke of his humanity. The logic of God is very simple. Since Adam, the 1st. man lost the authority over the earth, another man, Jesus, the last ADAM, had to get the authority back. IF God had come down to earth as God, then Lucifer would have had a valid reason to charge GOD with violating His own WORD.** God gave man dominion and not Himself, so even though Jesus was God before He Came to earth, He had to empty himself of his deity and could not act as God in any way while on earth.

JESUS BORN SINLESS\ADAM BORN INOCENT

Jesus and Adam both had the same authority and they both had to abide by the Old Testament Covenant (blood sacrificial system) (Genesis 4:1-5)(Matthew 8:1-4) So, they both spoke in the same authority under the same covenant of dominion.

(Gen.4:1-5) 'And Adam knew Eve his wife; and she conceived, and bare Cain, and said, I have gotten a man from the Lord. And she again bore his brother Able. And Able was a keeper of sheep, but Cain was a tiller of the ground. And in process of time it came to pass, that Cain brought of the fruit of the ground an offering unto the Lord. And Able, he also brought of the firstlings of his flock and of the fat thereof, and the Lord had respect unto Able and his offering. But unto Cain and his offering he had no respect. And Cain was very wroth (angry) and his countenance fell.' (His face looked very dejected).

Able brought the right offering (sacrifice in the right order of the season) Cain brought the wrong offering for the season. The Passover always comes before the first fruit offering (blood offering always comes before the grain offering)

This passage demonstrates that that the sacrificial covenant was already in place with Adam because an animal blood covering was performed by God to Provide a cover for the disobedience of Adam and his wife. It seems evident that God conveyed to Adam the requirement of the blood covenant and the importance of it. **ABLE did it in the right order and CAIN did not.**

(Matthew 8:1-4) 'When he (Jesus), was come down from the mountain, great multitudes followed him. And behold, there came a leper and worshipped him, saying, LORD if thou wilt, thou canst make me clean. And Jesus put forth his hand, and touched him, saying. I will; be thou clean. And immediately his leprosy was cleansed.' And, Jesus said to him See thou tell no man; but go thy way, show thyself to the priest, and offer the gift (animal sacrifice) that Moses commanded, for a testimony unto them.'

Now, since Adam and Jesus are comparable in the covenant God gave to man in their authority on the earth, other parts of scripture make more sense, such as the statement Jesus makes just before He left Earth to go back to The Father in heaven. **(**Matthew 28:18-20)

'And Jesus came and spoke unto them, saying, '**All power is given unto me in Heaven and in Earth. Go you therefore, and teach all nations, baptizing** them in the name of the FATHER, and THE SON, and THE HOLY GHOST: Teaching them to observe all things whatsoever I have commanded you: and, lo, I am with you always, even unto the end of the world (age). AMEN.'

Jesus 'statement that all power is given unto me in HEAVEN and EARTH is some—what perplexing to those who believe that Jesus acted as God in his earthly ministry and that's why he could do miracles because he was God on earth. If that were true, why **didn't Jesus do miracles after He was resurrected from the dead? Because, after His resurrection Jesus took back His Position in the God Head. That meant that God could not exercise authority on the earth as man. Jesus then delegates that (restored) authority to his apostles and tells them to TEACH THEM (men) TO OBSERVE ALL THINGS THAT I HAVE COMMANDED YOU.**

Then Jesus says, lo (look) I am with you always even till the end of the world (age) (the time period allotted until Jesus returns to rule and reign on Earth as LORD of LORDS and KING of KINGS)

Taken literally, **Jesus has left us (HIS CHURCH) to complete what He returned to us, HIS CHURCH, in SALVATION in AUTHORITY and in HEALING. If Jesus can be believed, and He can, then the Church needs a wake-up call. This would entail a massive Training in Righteousness and what it means.**

The definition of RIGHTEOUSNESS means RIGHT-STANDING before GOD. Everyone will RECEIVE RIGHT-STANDING BEFORE GOD WHEN they RECEIVE JESUS AS their LORD AND SAVIOR. (JESUS has made us RIGHTEOUS BY HIS SHED BLOOD). **Jesus said no man comes to the Father, but (except) by me.**

The knowledge of the word seemed to be so simple, however, I made up my mind to receive it and put it into practice. Now, understanding the word would mean that I had to **do what Jesus said to do. Since Most of what Jesus said to do is found in the New Testament, this became my goal. I had to learn everything Jesus said and did so that I would know how Jesus did it. Knowing how Jesus did what he did would allow me follow in Jesus foot-steps and do what He said to do.**

NOW THE QUEST BEGINS

Knowing and doing are different. Knowing requires knowledge, doing requires understanding and courage. I had acquired a certain amount of Word

Knowledge just as many Christians have. However, I was attempting to go from knowledge to doing. Somehow I knew that I would need courage, because I would be going against many long held traditions and customs. It would be easy to fall in to the comfort trap of status quo when opposition would arise. However, I was resolved to stand firm no matter the opposition. Come hell or high water, I would stand on the WORD clearly stated and simply received and steadfastly believed.

As with every journey, various priorities are set and survival items are needed from time to time to sustain one's self on the journey. In my journey, I found that I would need Truth to be my first priority. Second, will my understanding alter what God originally set-up to accomplish his purposes in creating man—kind. Since it is Biblical documentation that I look to as the original bench-mark to determine Truth and determine if I have violated God's purposes, I will start with laying a foundation for Biblical Truth and God's original purposes. My contention is that God's Truth is valid yesterday, today, and forever.

TRUTH

1. **THE 1ST. TRUTH IS THAT GOD LOVES HIS TOTAL CREATION. (John 3:16)**
2. **Who God loves, He corrects as an opportunity for repentance** (This includes all people (Psalms 11:7)
3. **God is no respecter of persons. (**There is no opportunity to charge **GOD of favoring one over another) (Acts 10:34)**
4. **God's time is different than man's time when expressing His love to His creation. (A day is with the LORD is as a thousand years) (2Peter 3:8)**
5. **God is just (fair) in all His ways. (Rev. 19:3)**
6. **God does not with-hold any good thing from His Children. Just as a father would not give his child a snake if they asked for a fish, our father in heaven knows how to give good gifts. (Matthew 7: 10)**
7. **God's judgments are His expressions of love in the eternity of time. (We live in a limited time space of 7,000 years, and we will return to God's original Heavenly order after the 7,000 years have been completed)**

TRUTH/ LOVE/ PURPOSE

God says, seek me early when I MAY BE FOUND—Ask and it will be given unto you, Seek and you shall find, knock, and it will be opened unto you. GOD WANTS US TO FIND HIM AND TELLS US HOW.

The following passage in (Matthew 6:27-34) gives us a needed picture of God's **love for us.**

'Which of you by taking thought can add one cubit unto his stature? And why take you thought for raiment? Consider the lilies of the field, how they grow, they toil not, neither do they spin; And yet I say to you, that even Solomon in all his glory was not arrayed like one of these. Wherefore, if God so clothe the grass of the field, which today is cast into the oven, shall He not much more cloth you, Oh you of little faith? Therefore take no thought, saying, what shall we eat? Or what shall we drink? Or say, wherewithal shall we be clothed? For after all these things do the gentiles seek, for your heavenly Father knows that you have need of all these things, But seek you first the kingdom of God, and his righteousness and all these things will be added unto you. Take therefore no thought for the morrow: for the morrow shall take thought for the things of itself. Sufficient unto the day is the evil thereof.

A continuation of God's purposes is seen in the book of (Matthew7; 1-12)

'Judge not, that you be not judged. For with what judgment you judge you shall be judged; and with what measure you give, it shall be measured to you again. And why behold thou the mote that is in your brother's eye, but consider not the beam in your own eye? You hypocrite, first cast out the beam out of your own eye; and then shall thou see clearly to cast out the mote out of your brothers eye. Give not that which is holy unto the dogs, neither cast you your pearls before swine, lest they trample them under their feet, and turn again and rend you. (V.7)Ask and it shall be given you; seek and you shall find; knock and it shall be opened unto you; for every one that asks receives; and he that seeks finds; and to him knocks it shall be opened.' Or what man is thereof you whom if his son ask bread, will give him a stone?

Or if he asks for a fish, will he give him a serpent? If then, being evil, know how to give good gifts unto your children, how much more shall your Father which is in heaven give good things to them that ask him? Therefore all things whatsoever things that men should do to you, do you even so to them; for this is the law and the prophets'

These Bible passages show us the love of God toward us and also his purposes for us. He gives care and direction. These passages have been tremendously encouraging to me as I have looked back to major influence on my journey to divine healing. These passages demonstrate that God is always willing to do us good and not evil. For me these scriptures put to rest the concept that God gives us some sickness, illness or disease to teach us something or correct something we might need to master. In commenting on 'when sickness, illness or disease comes to us, I know God did not send these things to us. They came from the Devil. God doesn't leave us there in the hands of the devil but has made prior provision for any—thing the devil can throw at us. It is called the **'kingdom of heaven'**. Jesus came to Earth to establish the Kingdom of Heaven on Earth through **man.** We know this by the prayer Jesus gave to the Disciples when teaching to pray.

'Our Father, who are in heaven, holy is your name, **(your) kingdom come, your will be done, on Earth, as it is in Heaven.'** (Matthew 6:9-10)

Another verse that Jesus gave to his disciples to point them in the proper direction was '**Seek you first** the **Kingdom of God** and **His Righteousness** and **all these things** will be **added unto you.'**(Matthew 6; 33)

For me to understand what God is saying in His word it was necessary for me to examine these words and see why God uses them.

- WHY SEEK?
- HOW SEEK?
- WHY FIRST?
- WHAT IS THE KINGDOM OF GOD?
- WHAT IS OUR ROLE IN THE KINGDOM OF GOD?
- WHAT IS GOD'S ROLE IN THE KINGDOM OF GOD?
- WHAT IS HIS RIGHTEOUSNESS?
- HOW DO WE GET HIS RIGHTEOUSNESS?

* To seek for a thing requires LOOKING for a thing—Jesus said to look (seek).

> * How to seek is to KNOW WHAT to seek for—Jesus said SEEK FOR the KINGDOM.
> *The first priority in the kingdom of God is to KNOW THAT IT EXISTS.
> *The Kingdom of God is A SPOKEN KINGDOM—we must MASTER (Bible) WORDS.
> *Our ROLE in the Kingdom is to SREAD IT AROUND so others my come in.
> *God's ROLE is to let all of His children know about the kingdom thru man. (BIBLICAL TEACHERS)
> *God's RIGHTOUSNESS is only available THRU JESUS, the perfect sacrifice.
> *We RECIEVE God's righteousness when VERBAL and public confession is
> Stated that Jesus is LORD and TOOK OUR SIN by the washing of His blood.

The objective of looking into the WORD OF GOD, (the BIBLE) is that we must decide if the Bible is true, accurate and dependable and verifies reality. If the Bible is not true we are wasting our time and we are beyond help in this life and the one to come.

Since it was God who made HIS Kingdom, it is God who made the rules on how His kingdom works.

If we misunderstand Gods' provisions, then we should know that the Consequences may be severe, and, un-necessary suffering may be the result. We must be in the right position to receive Gods' provision.

RIGHTEOUSNESS, Put simply means RIGHT-STANDING before GOD. There is no Sin that is not forgiven under the Grace of God. (Grace means that God has shown an un-merited favor towards us, we have done nothing to earn it) It is all because of the finished work of Jesus Christ on the Cross. With Righteousness, we are made ready to do the work of God, and do it without guilt. Fear and guilt from the past stops the work of the Righteous because Satan continually reminds us of our past failure and many of us fall for it.)

When we don't know who we are, we as men and women of God can be deceived into believing that we are still of the World. If we fall into that trap we will begin to follow those worldly patterns and habits. We begin to go after the things of the world and begin to think, that's who I am. Our goal becomes things and not God. Jesus corrects this thinking with his statement that puts us back on the right track. **(Seek you first the kingdom of God and His Righteousness and all these things will be added unto you)**

This will keep us in Right-standing before God. With clear knowledge of who we are, in Christ Jesus, we can then freely inter into the work of the Lord with joy and thanks—giving.

It is only when we know our right—standing before God that we can enter into the work that God has instructed us to do in the church and the world. For too long the Church has given the responsibility to the clergy to lead them in paths of works instead of paths of righteousness. When the church understands, right-standing before God, then it will move in power, confidence and boldness. It is about time that the Church wake—up and see her—self as God sees her.

CHAPTER 2

UNDERSTANDING

Since the Ways of God are beyond the ways of man, I do not believe that God intends that we ignore His ways. Or, even that we can—not understand the ways of God. Let me begin with three word group definitions. THOUGHTS/ WORD-THOUGHTS/ WORDS

1). **THOUGHTS ARE THE RESULT OF BEING DEVELOPED AS HUMAN BEINGS, THROUGH EXPERIENCE, EXPOSURE TO LANGUAGE AND STIMULATIONS IN THE INDIVIDUAL FROM THE INVIORNMENT. THOUGHTS MAY ORIGINATE FROM A PERSONS MIND OR COME TO US VIA THE AIR-Waves (Satan is said to be the Prince of the air-waves). THOUGHTS IN THE AIR-WAYS PRE-SUPPOSES, THAT, THERE IS A REALM THAT WE ARE EXPOSED TO BUT, ONE THAT WE CANNOT SEE. IN OTHER WORDS THERE IS AN UNSEEN WORLD OR ANOTHER DEMENSION THAT WE SENSE WITH OUR MIND.**

2). **WORD-THOUGHTS ARE THE ABILITY OF THE HUMAN MIND TO THINK IN PICTURES AND PUT MEANING TO THE PICTURE. WORD-THOUGHTS CAN ORIGINATE FROM A PERSONS OWN MIND OR FROM THE AIR-WAVES. WHEN WE THINK IN WORDS WE MAY HAVE THE IMPRESSION THAT WE ARE SPEAKING SILENTLY IN OUR MIND. THE REALITY IS, WE ARE ONLY THINKING WORD-THOUGHTS THAT GIVE BIRTH TO IDEAS. IDEAS ARE POWERLESS UNTIL SPOKEN.**

3). **WORDS ARE GOD CREATED SOUNDS WHICH CONVEY REALITY. (REALITY AND SUBSTANCE CARRY THE SAME**

MEANING). WORDS ARE THE BUILDING BLOCKS OF ALL CREATION AND ALL CREATED THINGS. THEREFORE, WORDS HAVE POWER AND MUST BE SPOKEN IN ORDER TO GIVE SUBSTANCE TO EVERY THING IN THE WORLD. (MANIFEST AND CONVEY CARRY THE SAME MEANING).

THE SPOKEN WORD

SINCE WORDS ARE THE CREATIVE BUILDING BLOCKS OF GOD, IT IS IMPARITIVE THAT EVERY CONSIDERATION BE GIVEN TO THEIR USE. IF USED WITH WISDOM OR MALICE, THEY HAVE THE SAME EFFECT.

- ❖ POWER TO CREATE / POWER TO DESTROY
- ❖ POWER TO HEAL / POWER TO CONVEY SICKNESS
- ❖ POWER TO TEACH / POWER TO KEEP IGNORANT
- ❖ POWER TO INFORM / POWER TO WITHHOLD
- ❖ POWER FOR TRUTH / POWER FOR LIES
- ❖ POWER FOR REVELATION / POWER FOR DECEPTION
- ❖ POWER TO GIVE AUTHORITY / POWER TO TAKE AUTHORITY
- ❖ POWER TO GIVE POWER / POWER TO TAKE POWER
- ❖ POWER TO GIVE DOMINION / POWER TO MAKE SUBMISSIVE

SPEAKING IS ESSENTIAL TO GOD'S KINGDOM
SPEAKING IS ESSENTIAL IN GOD'S KINGDOM
IN MY JOURNEY TO DIVINE HEALING I HAVE OBSERVED IN THE BIBLE, THAT IT APPEARS, THAT THE ONLY WAY GOD WORKS IN AND ON THE EARTH IS BY THE SPOKEN—WORD. IN ADDITION, IT ALSO APPEARS THAT A MAN MUST SPEAK IN ORDER FOR ANYTHING TO HAPPEN ON EARTH. THIS WOULD CONFIRM THAT ONCE GIVEN, DOMINION WAS NEVER TAKEN FROM MAN BY GOD AT ANY TIME. (PAST OR PRESENT)
SINCE MAN HAS DOMINION ON EARTH, GOD IS NOT IN CONTROL ON EARTH, MAN IS. This is a strange concept to some since most churches teach that God is always in control and nothing happens except by His permission. (anything good and anything bad.) If something good happens, God gets the credit, if it is bad God gets the blame.

I believe that the idea that GOD IS IN CONTROL makes for a complacent CHURCH. People will reason that since God is in control, why bother to make any extra effort to be obedient or make necessary changes since God is in control, whatever they do will not make a difference anyway. In addition, God gets unjustly blamed for the actions that people do through ignorance, mal-intentions or down-right hatefulness.

These concepts and provisions are developed for the sole purpose of assisting the Church (**God's People) to become the working body of Jesus on the Earth to the glory of God.** At the same time, the people of God are living in the careless use of words and suffering the un-intended consequences. Once God establishes or creates, He never goes back on His Word. From the time He speaks it, it is established or created. In the Day God made Adam, He established the order on earth for the way things are to function. God has not changed HIS MIND, and remains' the same yesterday, today and forever'. (Hebrews 13:8)

PRAYER AND THE SPOKEN WORD

As I define prayer in a Biblical context, it is the SPOKEN WORD TO GOD. Speaking is defined as verbal sounds whispered or said out loud. Therefore, prayer out loud is heard by GOD. When we pray in word-thoughts (in our mind) we are only thinking our prayer if do not speak.

GOD KNOWS OUR THOUGHTS, BUT NO-WHERE IN THE **BIBLE** DOES GOD EVER PROMMISE TO ANSWER OUR THOUGHTS. **GOD DOES SAY THAT HE WILL HE WILL HEAR AND ANSWER OUR CRY AND OUR PRAYER.** (Psalm 120:1) (Psalm 138:3) Prayer and crying to the Lord both require **words/sounds. In God's kingdom SPEAKING is ESSENTIAL to every part of God's creation.**

IN THE BOOK OF DANIEL THERE IS A PRIME EXAMPLE OF THE PRINCIPLE OF PRAYING OUT LOUD AND GOD'S PROVISION IN ANSWERING DANIEL.

"NOW WHEN DANIEL KNEW THAT THE DECREE WAS SIGNED, HE WENT INTO HIS HOUSE; AND THE WINDOWS BEING OPENED IN HIS CHAMBER TOWARDS JERUSELEM, HE KNEELED UPON HIS KNEES THREE TIMES A DAY, AND PRAYED AND GAVE THANKS BEFORE HIS GOD, AS HE DID AFORETIME." Then these men assembled, and found Daniel praying and making supplication before his God. (Daniel

6: 10) The question arises, how did the men know that Daniel was praying to his God? The answer is simple, Daniel was praying out-loud to his God. God heard Daniel pray and answered him.

Today the people of God are trained to think that God is going to answer their THOUGHT or MEDITATION. It is called SILENT PRAYER. This concept of silent prayer can be and is quite harmful. The effect is to make Gods' people passive and complacent. This is especially true when people who PRAY SILENTLY cannot put a clear answer from God to their UNSPOKEN REQUEST. At best, the silent prayer approach is a hit-and-miss or 50/50 chance that they might get a result by chance. The SILENT PRAYER approach also puts Gods' reputation on the line when people have not actually asked God Anything. God has never promised any—where in the BIBLE that HE will answer OUR SILENT THOUGHTS or MEDITATIONS. As a result people begin to seek out other people in the church TO PRAY FOR THEM BECAUSE THEY DON'T BELIEVE THAT GOD HEARS THEM, and they have had poor results and don'tknow why. This hit-and-miss approach also gives GOD the wrongful reputation that HE does not answer his Children when they pray. This then leads to the idea that God is a RESPECTER OF PERSONS and that HE is UNFAIR and CANNOT BE TRUSTED.

All of the above misguided ideas are are a result of Bad TEACHING, CHURCH TRADITIONS and CHURCH CUSTOMS. This can all be corrected with proper teaching and training

The Bible as the Word of God is replete with examples of speaking when praying and speaking with specific requests to God. One example often used to counter my position is the story of the Woman with the issue of blood for 12 years. It seems that in this account, at least two layers in her case needs to be examined. First, was the woman speaking the key to the woman's healing or second, was her action of touching the prayer shawl that JESUS was wearing the cause for her healing or was it a combination of both speaking and touching.

"And a certain woman which had an issue of blood twelve years, and had suffered many things of many physicians, and had spent all that she had, and was nothing bettered, but rather grew worse. When she had heard of JESUS, came in the press behind, and touched his garment. For she said, If, I may touch but his clothes, I shall be made whole". (Mark5:25-30)

"And straightaway the fountain of her blood was dried up; and she felt in her body that she was healed of the plague. And JESUE immediately knowing in himself that virtue had gone out of Him, HE turned about in the press and said "Who touched my clothes?" 'and his disciples said unto him, Thou see the multitude thronging thee, and you say, Who touched me ? And he looked around to see her that had done this thing. But the woman fearing and trembling, knowing what was done in her she came before him and told him all the truth. And HE SAID UNTO HER, *DAUGHTER, THY FAITH HATH MADE THEE WHOLE; GO IN PEACE, AND BE WHOLE OF THY PLAGUE* (Mark5:25-34) The remarkable thing about JESUS referring to this woman as *DAUGHTER* is that this implies that she is in HIS FAMILY AND THEREFORE ENTITLED TO HEALING. Are we not also in Gods' family and entitled to HIS PROVISIONS.

The point and focus of the above is *faith and covenant. The woman had to exercise her faith by reaching out and touching the garment of Jesus.* However, what ignited the woman's faith was an old-testament verse in the book of (Malachi 4:2) which says, "*But unto you that fear my name SHALL THE SON OF RIGHTEOUSNESS ARISE WITH HEALING IN HISWINGS;* "And you shall go forth and grow-up as calves of the stall ". She first spoke faith, then, she made a claim on what the *SCRIPTURE SAID* she could. She then reached out and touched and she was *HEALED.* The garment that Jesus wore was a *PRAYER—SHAWL* and the promise was that the *CORNERS* were called *WINGS AND CONSISTED OF LONG TASSELES THAT HUNG DOWN BEYOND THE BOTTOM BOARDER OF THE GARMENT.* The woman JOINED her FAITH and HER KNOWLEDGE of her COVENENT and *RECEIVED HER HEALING WHEN SHE REACHED OUT AND TOUCHED THE GARMENT OF JESUS.*

CONCLUSION/SUMMARY

If we as the Church of JESUS CHRIST are to thrive in a world which is badly in need of answers, solutions and results, we must know our covenant. Knowing your covenant (which is knowledge) is the first step. Doing what the covenant requires is the second step. Since *JESUS IS OUR EXAMPLE FOR DOING EVERYTHING HE TOLD US TO DO. THIS MEANS THAT, JESUS IS, PERFECT THEOLOGY.* You need only to read the 1st four books of the New Testament; Matthew, Mark, Luke, and John, in-order to understand what Jesus did and how He did it. If we are to be authentic effective Christians, we must learn to use our words like a skilled carpenter, just as Jesus did. This requires a dedication to knowing the truth. The Bible says, in the words of

Jesus, "*I am the way, the truth and the Life. No one comes to the father but by me (*John 14:6) This statement by Jesus is absolute and cannot be equivocated.

If we are to be effective and thrive in faith, we must learn the lesson of the woman with the issue of blood and really know our *covenant and how to access it.* After all we have a *better new Covenant according to* (Hebrews 8:6) It is well to note here that *Jesus had to do everything from the Old Testament covenant provisions.*

Our better COVENANT includes TWO KEY elements, FAITH and SPEAKING. "FAITH comes by HEARING and HEARING BY THE WORD OF GOD" (Romans 10:17) In addition, "FAITH without works IS DEAD". (James 2:17) Both the Old and the New Covenant requires people of faith to do something observable to demonstrate or activate their faith. SPEAKING was established in (GENESIS 1:4)) as the way God brought everything into being and it has never been changed in Gods' Word, the Bible. *Speaking, is established in the Book of Genesis as the way God made all of creation.* In all of Scripture, this principle of speaking things into bring has not been nullified as God's creative principle.

There are those in the Faith that are subject to some misconception about what they understand about SPEAKING things into BEING. They say things like "those people who *name it and claim it, and blab it and grab it. are way out there* They seem to think that by putting down those who believe that a person who speaks with expectation that GOD will answer their prayer are some—how short in the mental department. I believe that SATAN would like nothing better than to put Christians off of the PRINCPLE OF SPEAKING THE PROVISIONS OF GOD Because he knows that is where THE POWER IS.

In general, the church has many traditions that have worked against what the word of God says. Some, if not all, seem to have the following type of statement, 'We don't do things like that around here'. 'We have always done it like this.' They preach from the Old Testament as though all of it applies to the Church today.' What the leadership in the church seems to have taken on for themselves is the mantel of responsibility for weather the church is performing what Jesus commissioned us to do. It seems that too many times it is mans interpretation of what someone in a leadership position decides rather than what the BIBLE explicitly states. Many Seminaries who train pastors for service in their denominations are guilty of this practice and are under-preparing those they send out to serve.

CHAPTER 3

WAS JESUS GOD

The answer to the question, was Jesus God? I believe has a three part answer—YES, NO, YES. This is not a trick answer, but it does need an explanation from the Bible. Also, the answer to this question will answer many other questions in the Bible that the Saints often misunderstand, and therefore we stumble at obeying what Jesus told us to do before He went back into Heaven.

1) YES-Jesus was GOD before He was came to Earth to be the Savior of the world. (John 1:1-18) "In the beginning was the Word, and the Word was with God, and the Word was God. The same was in the beginning with God. All things were made by him; and without him was not anything made that was made".... v.18 "No man has seen God at any time; the only begotten Son, which is in the bosom of the Father, he has declared him".

2) NO—Jesus voluntarily emptied self of His deity in order to fulfill the requirement of God's created order of giving Man authority on earth. (Genesis 1:26-27) "And God said, Let us make man in our own image, after our likeness: and let them have dominion over the fish of the sea, and over the fowl of the air, and over the cattle, and over all the earth, and over every creeping thing that creeps on the earth". V.27" So God created man in his own image, in the image of God created he him; male and female created he them". Jesus died as a man, went down to Hell and announced to the underworld that the power of Satan was broken over mankind, and man's authority is restored to him. Jesus did this as man. 'Son of man' a name Jesus gave himself (Matthew 8:20).

3) YES—JESUS, BEING RAISED from the dead fulfilled the sacrificial blood covenant to restore to man his rightful place on Earth and frees

Jesus to take His rightful place in the God Head. Notice that JESUS did no mighty healing works after he was on earth for forty days after his raising from the dead. After the forty days were ended, Jesus ascended on high, having given instructions to his disciples to go into the world and do the work that they are now equipped to do. However, they were to wait for the Power of God to come and empower them. (Pentecost) fifty days after the Jesus was crucified. (Acts 1:8) "But you shall receive power, after that the Holy Spirit is come upon you: and you shall be my witnesses unto me both in Jerusalem, and in all Judaea and Samaria, and unto the uttermost part of the earth".

The intent of my comparing the three points above is to demonstrate that JESUS emptied himself from being God in Heaven before he came to earth so could not act as GOD when HE took a physical body in the form of man. He did this in order to avoid violating the original command of God. When God said, let man have dominion, 'He meant it. And in addition, there is nothing in the Bible that says that GOD ever changed His mind. Therefore Jesus had to become a Man under the original design of God, born of a woman's seed.

MY WORLD VIEW

My view of the world was influenced more by the question of, 'was Jesus God during his earthly ministry' than any other factor in my journey to divine healing. Once I looked at biblical evidence and was fully persuaded that the logic of God in sending Jesus to **restore to mankind that which lost, the rest was just a matter of diligent study of the Bible.**

Since **Jesus is perfect theology, his life provides us the perfect example of what He expects of those who follow him. The first** revelation to me was that Jesus was a Jew and that his life and foundations lay in the Jewish experience. I remembered an Old Testament verse that said 'to the Jew first, and also to the gentile' (Romans 1:16; 2:9-10) which started me to thinking, that most churches don't take that verse to heart as a priority of **God towards the Jewish people. Since it is a priority of God, I decided that it would be my priority towards the Jewish people. Another verse reinforced my view when I read in (Genesis 12:3) 'And I will bless them that bless thee, and curse him that curse thee; and in thee shall all families of the earth be blessed'. God has never taken this statement back or repented of it. Therefore, I can only take it that His word is**

still good and He will bless those who bless the Jewish People and curse those who curse the Jewish People. History bears witness.

Another question arises out of the same concern that Jesus was or was not-God during His earthly ministry. That question is 'could Jesus yield to temptation or be tempted if he was God while on earth'? If Jesus was God: He could not act as God because he would have violated the authority originally given to man. According to James1:13-20, "let no man say when he is *tempted, I am tempted of God:* for *God cannot be tempted with evil* neither *tempts he any man"* On the other hand (Hebrews 4:15-16) clearly states, "Seeing that we have a great high Priest that has passed into the Heavens, *Jesus The Son of God.* Let us hold fast to our (faith) profession".v.16 reads, "For we have not a High Priest which cannot be touched with the *feeling of our infirmities; but was in all points tempted* like as we are, *Yet without sin"*

When Jesus 'ministry began, He was baptized in the river Jordan, and straightway he was driven into the desert where he was *tempted* of the devil after he fasted for (40) forty days. It is interesting that Jesus never took on Satan as God, but referred to the Old Testament scripture, just as we are required to do in the New Testament. This tells the Church, that Jesus, as *a man in the flesh*, a real flesh and blood man, who had to overcome all of the same temptations and pitfalls as we in the world must face as a result of a fallen human family because of sin. According to (1 Cor.15:22) in Adam, all die. However, in (1 Cor.15:45) Jesus is referred to as *the LAST* ADAM indicating that, there will be no other Adam after Jesus. If man was to be redeemed, everything was on the line in the garden when Jesus was faced with *the decision of the ages. Shall Jesus succeed where the First Adam failed. Or will mankind live forever in Sin.*

Thankfully, Jesus made the best decision for mankind and was *obedient to the Plan and Will of GOD.* The same decision Jesus made is the same decision we are called to make when we are *rebellious* or *obedient* to Gods" Plan of Salvation.

Jesus had freewill just as we have freewill, the difference being that Jesus fully understood the consequences of his decision for man-kinds eternal future. Typically, we as Gods' children don't take the view Jesus took in exercising our freewill. We are mostly taken with the idea that our freewill is for our benefit only, if someone is close to us they may also benefit. In our human nature our short-term view is the one that usually prevails. However, God has called us to a higher calling than that of simply satisfying our own needs. The Bible says "greater love has no man, than to lay down his live for his fellow man". In this statement is the entire life of Jesus wrapped-up. *Since Jesus' life is Perfect Theology we would do well to follow Him in all of His ways and leave the result to Him.* Jesus will not lead us astray. He will *lead us in paths of righteousness for his Name sake. His rod and His staff (power and protection) will comfort us. He will make room for us in the middle of our enemies camp and feed us. Surely the angels of goodness and mercy shall follow me all the days of my life and I shall dwell in the House of The LORD forever.*

The power of WORDS

Those of Jesus 'day spoke of him as speaking with great authority. The people who observed Jesus do great miracles and do many healings, were impressed with the wonder of this man who could do such things. They comented, 'is not this the son of Mary and Joseph 'And from where does he get his power'. It seems that Jesus was well aware of the power of words as a man. Since Jesus is our example it then follows that we should equate our-selves in the same way. We should know that words are the building blocks of our lives. We also may work miracles, heal the sick, cast out demons, raise the dead or any other command Jesus gave to us to do. The main obstacle to the body of Christ Jesus (the church) in doing what we are instructed, is unbelief and training. Most Christians are dependent on others to pray for them. They are still baby's in their behaviors and have not grown up to take solid food. This means that they have not been able to read the Bible for them-selves and digest it for them-selves. Tradition has shown that as a church body, we have depended mostly upon the pastors and teachers to give us the answers we seek. In many cases, the answers have been unreliable or incomplete when people are looking for results.

JESUS said' I am the *way,* the *truth*, and the *life,* no one comes to the *Father, but by me'.* And again he said in another place' *My words are SPIRIT and they are LIFE.*

All we need do is to follow the words of JESUS and then DO THEM. Leave the results to Him He will not let you down. It has been my experience that, the more I trust in HIM, his WAYS, HIS WORD, He shows up strong and up-holds his WORD, his WAYS and his NAME. Our role as Christians is to preach the gospel and signs will follow us. It makes no difference if you are old or young, big or small, short or tall, because JESUS is not a respecter of persons. In the next example we will take look at the Words of Jesus about sowing seed on various types of soil.

Matthew 13:1-9 States, The same day went Jesus out of the house, and sat by the sea side. And great multitudes were gathered together unto him, so that he went into a ship, and sat; and the whole multitude stood on the shore. And he spoke many things unto them in **parables, saying, '***Behold a man went forth to sow; And when he sowed, some seeds fell by the way side, and the fouls came and devoured them up; Some fell upon stony places where they had not much earth; and forthwith they sprung up, because they had no deepness of earth; And when the sun was up, they were scorched; and because they had no root, they withered way. And some fell among thorns; and the thorns sprung up, and chocked them; But, other fell on good ground and brought forth fruit, some an hundredfold, some sixty fold, some thirtyfold.* **Who hath ears to hear, let him hear'** And the disciples came and said to him, why speakest thou unto them in parables? (Matthew 13:10) He answered and said unto them. *Because it is given unto you know the mysteries of the kingdom of heaven, but to them it is not given.*

There are two passages to pay strict attention to in order to fully understand what JESUS is conveying to his disciples.

1). **GOOD GROUND AND BROUGHT FORTH FRUIT, SOME THRITY FOLD SOME, SIXTY FOLD, SOME HUNDRED FOLD.**
2). **BECAUSE IT IS GIVEN UNTO YOU TO KNOW THE MYSTERIES OF THE KINGDOM OF HEAVEN,**

THE QUESTION ON # 1) IS WHY then is there A DIFFERENCE IN THE WAY *GOOD GROUND* PRODUCES FRUIT. WHY 100 FOLD, 60 FOLD, 30 FOLD?

THE QUESTION ON # 2) IS WHAT IS THE MYSTRY OF THE KINGDOM OF HEAVEN WE SHOULD KNOW?

With a close examination of these two issues, I believe we will find a surprising answer and a new and old revelation from the Holy Spirit.

As Jesus so often did, in the book of Matthew, JESUS answers the second question first. So I will follow his lead and follow with (Matthew 13: 11) "Because it is given unto you to know the mysteries of the kingdom of heaven, *but to them it is not given. For whoso ever hath, to him shall be given, and he shall have more abundance; but whosoever hath not, from him shall be taken away even that he hath. Therefore speak I to them in parables; because they seeing see not; and hearing they hear not, neither do they understand.* And in them is fulfilled the prophecy of Elijah (E-sai-as), which says, *By hearing ye shall hear and not understand; and seeing ye shall see and not preceive:*

For this people's heart is waxed gross, and their ears are dull of hearing, And their eyes they have closed; lest at any time they should see with their eyes, and should understand with heart, and should be converted, and I should convert them. BUT BLESSED ARE YOUR EYES, FOR THEY SEE: AND YOUR EARS, FOR THEY HEAR. *For verily I say unto you, That many prophets and righteous men have desired to see those things which you see, and have not seen them; and hear those things which ye hear and have not heard them."*

THE MYSTERY OF THE KINGDOM

Since the Kingdom of Heaven was offered to the Jewish people first and was a priority of Jesus in his first coming, this puts an enlightened view on why Jesus said what he said. Once the Jewish Nation of Israel rejected Jesus' offer of the Kingdom, they became blind to their Heritage of the Kingdom. It was a self imposed Blindness. However, Jesus states that when Israel sees with their eyes and hears with their ears HE SHOULD VONVERT THEM AND HEAL THEM.

The misconception is that because Israel did not keep covenant with God and therefore lost their rightful heritage, and, that God gave them up as His people and turned to the church in order to fulfill the prophecies that concern Israel. Well, on May 14, 1948, that concept was dispelled with the rebirth of Israel. Israel is back in the land that God gave them and God is restoring Israel to their rightful place in their land. They will never leave again.

What Jesus is saying in the The Mystery of The Kingdom to the Jewish Nation is that when they HAVE EARS TO HEAR AND UNDERSTAND THE GOSPEL AND EYES TO SEE AND UNDERSTAND WHAT THEY ARE LOOKING AT IN HIM, THEN He will be obligated to HEAL AND CONVERT them and restore the KINGDOM TO THEM. This is HIS PROMISE TO THEM.

ANSWER TO QUESTION # 1—THE PARABLE OF THE SOWER

(Matthew 13: 18-23) Hear ye therefore the parable of the sower. (learn what it means) When anyone hears the word of the kingdom, and understands it not, then the wicked one comes and catches that which was sown in his heart. This is he which received seed by the way side. But he that received the seed into stony places, the same is he that hears the word, and with joy receives it; Yet he has no root in himself, endures for a while: for when tribulation or persecution arises because of the word, by and by he is offended. He also that received seed among the thorns is he that hears the word; and the cares of this world, and the deceitfulness of riches, choke the word, and he becomes unfruitful. But he that receives seed into the good ground is he that hears the word, and understands it; which also bears fruit, and brings forth, some one hundred fold, some sixty fold, some thirty fold.'

For years it appeared that the reference to *hundred fold, sixty fold, and thirty fold was a reference to 100 percent, 60 percent and 30percent of* production from the seed put on the good soil. That does not make sense if the quality of the soil is *all good which the seed goes into. The soil which is good should all produce the same percentage of increase.* It is only when we see that the seed is the WORD OF GOD, that we can make clear sense of the parable and the intent of Jesus in using the parable. *First, the seed is the gospel, and the gospel is characterized as 'good news'.*

In recent years (twenty five) I have come to the conclusion that the Gospel (good news) consists of three **parts**:

> *SALVATION:* is the gift of God to man (man—kind) by a blood covenant through JESUS OF NAZARETH THE LAST ADAM. (1 cor.15:45)

> *HEALING AND RESTORATION* : Man is restored to his original state of well being as in the garden of Eden. (By His stripes we are healed) (Isaiah 53:3-6).

> *AUTHORITY AND DOMINION :* JESUS restored our authority and dominion when he said the words 'it is finished'. He completed the total mission his father sent him to do as 'son of man' Jesus death completed his earthly legal transaction to get back what Satan stole from mankind. Satan stole mans legal authority over the earth, Jesus returned it to him legally,' for the Son of man is come to save that which was lost'. (Matthew 18:11).

When only one of the three parts of the gospel is preached and the other two parts are neglected, that Church will only get 30 FOLD fruit RETURN on that WORD PREACHED. *WHEN TWO of THE THREE parts of the Gospel are Preached, that THE CHURCH WILL GET A 60 FOLD FRUIT RETURN. When all three parts of the gospel is preached, that Church will get a 100 fold fruit return on the Word Preached.* **THE COMPLETE GOOD NEWS**

Many Churches experience members who moved from church to church in search of all three parts of Gods' gospel preached.

Many church members do not even know why they are going from church to church. All they know is that something is not being given to them. The result is lowering their expectations. They begin to feel uncared for and they then begin to wonder around in search of another church, or worse, they simply stay at home.

When we are not taught the full message of the gospel, we are deficient in our performance of the Word. Another way of saying, we just don't do it. On the other hand, if those brave souls who attempt to do the word with insufficient knowledge, the results will be lacking and the people of God are discouraged.

SALVATION—HEALTH/HEALING—AUTHORITY/DOMINION

The keys to the kingdom of GOD operate under the LAWS, PROVISIONS, PRECEPTS and STATUES established by God when HE set up the KINGDOM. If we are unaware of Gods' set up we are easy prey for the Evil One. He will lie and blame God.

THE THREE FOLD COMPLETE GOSPEL IS OUR PROTECTION AGAINST ALL OF LIFE'S CIRCUMSTANCES AND AGAINST EVERY THING THE ENEMY CAN THROUGH AT US. IF WE ARE WISE WE WILL ENTER INTO THEIR PROTECTIVE COVER and PROVISION.

Before we go further, let me explain the importance of the order of the three—part Gospel. FIRST, SALVATION is the the beginning point of everything that God uses to draw man into the KINKDOM. SECOND, HEALING is where most people live and have concerns. If KINGDOM people are sick and weak, they do not make a good example for Gods' people to follow. THIRD, AUTHORITY is the provision which is set-up to operate the effectiveness of SALVATION and HEALING.

WORDS THAT ARE SPOKEN AND WRITTEN ARE BINDING

God is a legal God. Which is to say that what—ever God says is binding on what it is spoken into. If a parent speaks negative things into their child, that child will reflect that negative word in behavior or words. Conversely, If that parent speaks positive words into their child, there will be a positive result in words or behavior. Since GENESIS 1:26 tells us that we are made in the image of God, our words are just as binding on whatever we speak into also. This is a principle of behavior which God set up at the very beginning in establishing the parameters under which His kingdom WORKS and man's place in it. This principle is not expressed more clearly than in the 23rd. Psalms which clearly in the prayers given to the Apostles. "Our father who is in heaven, holy is thy name. Your will be done, thy kingdom come on EARTH as it is in HEAVEN." The intent is clearly is to have God's Kingdom in heaven be reflected here on Earth.

In all legal matters here on Earth, there are written or verbal agreements which are binding. Heaven is also a place of written and verbal agreements. They are just as binding. When God said in (Genesis 1; 26) "let us make man in our own image" that was a legal and binding statement by God concerning all men and women. All we need do in all scripture is to look for the LEGAL language that God uses when He makes any statement in the Bible. When we read the Bible we receive statements made from God by His prophets, angels, and apostles, all of which are spoken as though directly from God. All His promises are true and sure, weather spoken by God or a true spokesman.

God is a legal God, Which is to say that God abides by his own agreements which He has established. This is why some feel that God lets bad things happen to people and that God won't rescue them when they step away from God's protective provisions. Often, God can—not step into a rescue situation until a correct word is spoken over that special situation.

CHAPTER 4

REPLACEMENT THEOLOGY

On my journey to divine healing, the question arises, should I put my whole trust in the Old Testament or the New Testament. Maybe I should trust both equally. After all Jesus lived and quoted the Old Testament in virtually every-thing from the Old Testament. All of his healing work was done under Old Testament Covenant provisions. All of his miracles were performed under Old Testament provisions. However, the Bible says that we have a New and better covenant than the Old covenant. (Hebrews 9:6-7) "But now hath he obtained a more excellent ministry, by how much also he is the mediator of a better covenant, which was accomplished upon better promises. For if that first covenant had been faultless, then should no place have been sought for the second." Did this mean that God had discarded the Jewish People because He had a better covenant through Jesus' death on the Cross? THE ANSWER IS NO.

Some—how the teaching in the Church determined that because the Jewish people were taken away in captivity and were no longer in a position to fulfill the promises that God had predicted in His prophecies about them, He was finished with them. This left the work of bringing the gospel to the world un—fulfilled. NATURALLY, SINCE THE COMMISION TO THE FIRST CHURCH (Jewish Church in Jerusalem) could no longer be accomplished, the Church believed it had a mandate to step-in and fulfill the Great Commission. (Matthew 24:14) "And this gospel OF THE KINGDOM shall be preached in all the world for a WITNESS UNTO ALL NATIONS and THEN THE END SHALL COME" This specific commission was given to the Jewish people, not the Church. God is not waiting for the Church to fulfill this Commission before returning to earth to set up His KINGDOM ON EARTH.

HOWEVER, THE JEWISH PEOPLE WILLFULFILL THIS THE GREAT COMMISSION. This promise will be kept when the Hundred-forty—four thousand, twelve thousand from each tribe as specified in (Revelation 6:4)

"And I heard the number of them which were sealed: and there were sealed an hundred and forty four thousand of all the tribes of the children Israel."

The church is not to be faulted because of the historic teaching that the Church replaced the Jewish people in Gods' plan of redemption of mankind. This is all they knew at the time. The idea that the church would make a difference in the lives of future generations would serve man—kind well and motivated many missionaries through-out the intervening years. This was all to the good. Thankfully, when MAY 14, 1948 CAME INTO VIEW AND ISRAEL BECAME A NATION AGAIN AFTER MORE THAN 1800 YEARS OUT OF THE LAND THAT GOD GAVE TO ABRAHAM, SOME IN THE CHURCH BEGAN TO READ THE BIBLE WITH NEW EYES. They began to make the connection that Israel had promises that were specific to Israel and that there are promises to the church that apply specifically to the church. The wonderful part about this is I remember when all this got started and my vivid impressions at the time.

It was in the mid 1960s that my awareness was peaked and I began to pursue Spiritual things in an active way. My young life was filled with church and bible reading. I can remember reading the Bible as a boy under the covers of my bed with a flash-light. Bible stories always fascinated me. I would imagine that I could do many of the things I read about if given the chance and God would back—me—up. At 12 years old, (1950) I received Jesus Christ as my Personal savior. This experience and commitment was emotional and lasting. The week before my public acceptance of Jesus, the Church showed a movie by Cecil B. De Mill, called KING OF KINGS', it was a silent movie with reading under the picture. I remember thinking, I'm glad I can read. However, looking back I believe it was the vivid pictures that helped me really see what Jesus really did for me. That, along with the knowledge that I was a sinner and had fallen short many, many times in my short life, I was convicted and surrendered to JESUS.

In the Baptist Church any conversion is always a matter of PUBLIC confession and WITNES. There was no closet 'come to Jesus moments' as you pray silently in your seat and pray later with someone who may or may not know the right

WORD to salvations and requirement for full assurance that you are saved, JESUS said," If you are ashamed of me before men, THEN I WILL BE ASHAMED OF YOU BEFORE THE FATHER". I BELIEVE THAT THE Baptist got it RIGHT. This is not to say that they don't need to improve in other areas of the Gospel.

Around 1967, the Christian world began to experience a new way in how they viewed the bible. On the one hand some had the view that the bible should be taken literally, especially since Israel had become a nation again. On the other hand, many still believed that in those parts which connected to Israel should be categorized as allegorical and not given any new serious consideration. I came into the camp that said that we should re-think all of our previous assumptions and re examine Scripture in light of the re—existence as a re-established nation of Israel. For me, the idea that Israel should be treated as allegorical was just plain ignorance on the part of those who would ignore all Bible—Prophecy, Psalms, Genesis and the book of Revelation. It was during this time period that I became firmly satisfied that I was on the right track.

Another major factor in my understanding that the Jews were still on Gods' major agenda was that JESUS WAS A JEW. Now I had to ask the question, if Jesus was a Jew, and he is coming back to rule and reign on the earth, why would a Loving God discard the very people He sent His Son to save first.

The oldest argument why many believe that the JEWS HAVE BEEN REPLACED is that of Plain old ANTI-SEMETISM. It is hard to understand but some people just hate the JEWS. They say why they hate Jews is that 'the Jews killed Jesus.' I notice that these are the same people who don't follow Jesus either.

During this re-awakening the PENTACOSTAL, the CHARISMATIC, the CHURCH OF GOD IN CHRIST, THE First church of GOD IN CHRIST, the BELIEVERS VOICE OF VICTORY, the CRENSHAW CHRISTIAN CENTER as well as such TELEVISION MINISTRIES as Benny Hinn, Don Stuart, Le Roy Jenkins, Fred Price, Catherin Coleman and many others, played a vital role.

It goes with—out saying, that the news media has formed an opinion about each of the influential men mentioned above and their opinion is not favorable. Worse yet, the mainline Church denominations view the above mentioned men and their work as heresy in many cases. From my study of the matter, I concluded that often the teaching of one or more of above described men of God may vary in a minor point, but certainly the label of apostate does not apply. The news media is not the only misinformed group concerning the CHURCH. Many times, it is the church itself that puts forth misinformation about ministers and ministries which do not agree with their brand name. I call this DENOMINATIONALISM. This is just another way of saying that the Baptists, the Methodist, the Catholics, the Mormons, the Church of God and a host of other Churches all believe that THEIR WAY IS BEST at the exclusion of all the others. Instead of working together to spread the gospel in unity, each grouping works in disharmony with each other. Instead of working in the unity of love, often it is working in isolation.

In the Book of REVLATION, Chapters 1-3, we see that God reviews seven (7) churches, each of which is inspected and given a commendation and a warning except the Church of PHILADELPHIA WHICH IS EXEMPT FROM A WARNNING. The reason is made clear in the reason why they are exempt. It is because the Church of Philadelphia does two things; they keep HIS NAME and HIS WORD. Then God tells them He will put no other requirement on them. In addition, God states that he will keep THEM FROM THAT HOUR OF TEMPTATION WHICH IS COMING ON THE WHOLE WORLD. This is the time of the TRIBULATION WHEN EVERY ONE WILL BE REQUIRED TO TAKE THE MARK OF THE BEAST OR BE BE-HEADED.

If the Church, as a total would preach the Total WORD of GOD as truth and Honor the NAME of JESUS in all that the Church does, then unity would come and escape from the wrath to come could be THEIRS. As it stands, some of the Church will go through the TRIBULATION Period. (REVELATION 6:11).

Replacement—Theology Confusion

The ideas about how the church came to be the center of all biblical scripture as it applies to application of the ol testament promises and covenant, and replaced the original intent that the Hebrews (Jews) somehow forfeited the original covenant promise. These ideas stem from some basic assumptions that if followed will lead us into what I see as some error in interpretation in the following scriptural areas.

1. The RAPTURE of the CHURCH—is it—before or after TRIBULATION
2. The SECOND coming of JESUS—is it—for the church or Judgment

3. The BLESSINGS of ABRAHAM—is it—to the Jew first or Church first

4. The GIFTS of 1Corintians 12:1-31—are they active in the Church today

5. Was JESUS GOD or was he A JEWISH MAN.—what did Jesus call himself

6. APPLING old Testament SCRIPURE—PRIMARILY to the CHURCH

7. BECOMING complacent—Just WAITING for GOD to save them

8. LOOKING for Gods' will for your life—is it—LITTLE emphasis on New Testament APPLICATION on what God has ALREADY TOLD US to do.

9. The Church not supportive of the Jewish Nation—is it—they are uncaring

10. Some in the Church believe that the Jews should be persecuted because of WHAT THEY THINK the JEWS DID to Jesus. Or, is it that the church is ignorant about what WE ALL DID to cause Jesus to have to come to Earth as a man and make an ATONEMENT for All of us.

God calls the people of Israel 'a peculiar people, a chosen nation'. Let us examine what this really means. First of all, Abram was called out of UR of the CALDEANS, a place of idols and idolatry, today called IRAQ. As Abram heard and went to the place of obedience that God sent him, he was given revelations about himself, his people, their future and their blessing to the Jew first and also to the Nations. The following is a direct Biblical reference to the original statement to Abram by God that sets in motion every—thing that should be understood concerning Israel. Read carefully the following passages.

(Genesis 12:1-4) "Now the LORD had said unto Abram, get thee out of thy country, and from thy kindred, and from thy fathers' house, unto a land that I will show thee. And I will make of thee a great nation, and I will bless thee, and will make thy name great; and thou shall be a blessing: And I will bless them that bless thee, and curse them that curse thee: and in thee shall all the families of the earth be blessed". According to the bible, there are no other people on earth THAT have been given this promise. THIS MAKES THE JEWISH PEOPLE A PECULIAR PEOPLE and A CHOSEN NATION.

When the church short circuits the complete relationship with the JEWISH NATION and people, it is the church and the Jewish people that are cut off from the blessings of God. It is my hope that my words in this book will ignite the church to a more loving, caring, respectful body of Jesus Christ towards the Jewish NATION and PEOPLE.

When I began to see the Jewish people as Jesus saw them in the four gospels account, my eyes were opened as I began to see how each of the gospel writers viewed Jesus' treatment of his very own people. This opened my understanding beyond measure. Jesus had such compassion and love in everything he did with the Jewish people. If I was to follow Jesus, I would have to revise what I had heard and been indoctrinated with. The indoctrination was subtle and indirect. Comments like, 'You know how Jews killed Jesus,' I don't need to support them. Or, THEY are into everything and THEY control EVERYTHING. Once attitudes are put in unchallenged verbal forms, most people are reluctant to speak up or put forth an opposing view. In this regard the Church is no different than the society at large. I believe that the Church must wake up if we are to reap the promise related to the RIGHT relationship with the Jews and Israel. The Bible says in very clear terms, 'I will bless those that bless thee and curse those that curse thee and in thee shall all the families of the earth be blessed,'(Matthew 12:3)

MATTHEW THE KEY

The key for me was the revelation that the book of MATTHEW was the main entry—point for understanding, as to how we as Christians are to move into the provision and right standing that Jesus gave us with His death on the cross. The book of Matthew was a blueprint directly from God which told me just what my limitations and provisions are under the New Testament covenant. To begin with, MATTHEW is written and addressed to the children of Israel. Second, the birth-right of Jesus to be the ONE who would deliver the children of Israel from their sins is established. Third, all of the Old Testament prophecy was fulfilled in the life of JESUS.

THE KINGDOM OF GOD KEY

The Kingdom of God is introduced in the book of Matthew in a three part way. First, Jesus describes the Kingdom of God in parables. Jesus then looks at the Kingdom of God from a functional point of view, a practical point of view and a literal point of view. In short Jesus shows us how the kingdom of God works in every day ways. In the latter part of Matthew, Jesus reveals how the Kingdom of God will be established in Jerusalem as the center of mans Earthly connection to JESUS. The Kingdom of God was the KEY to my understanding, the opening of Knowledge and, the sealing of wisdom to my heart for my function as one of Gods men for healing.

In order for me to understand a thing, I must have an example with which to Make a comparison to something I am already familiar with. This is the Foundation on which Jesus rested all of his PARABLES, FUNCTIONAL POINT OF VIEW, PRACTICAL POINT OF VIEW AND LITERAL POINT OF VIEW of everything He taught in the book of MATTHEW.

As we think of The Kingdom of God, traditional thoughts come to the mind of most people which thinks, 'the kingdom of God is in Heaven, and I am looking forward to getting there'. However, JESUS said 'the Kingdom of God is at hand'. My understanding of this statement is that, the kingdom is here Right Now. It was this revelation that pushed me into the here-and-now behavior that Jesus expects of us as His people. It was this knowledge that spurred me into action.

Generally people want to do the right thing, if for no other reason than to appear to be in the right place doing the right thing. That is all well and good if for no other reason than that it keeps a lot of people out of mischief. It also reduces the chance for people doing something wrong, and this is a good thing. I believe that this thought was in Paul's mind when he wrote'. Do not neglect to gather yourselves together, as is the habit of some'. Paul is speaking of some in the church that stay away from church at their own peril. However, WHEN the people are taught the full gospel of Jesus Christ, then the people who come to church will find a continuing growth potential and will come to learn about the Kingdom. The Church on the other hand must be prepared TO TEACH THE WHOLE WORD AS TRUTH and have a bible basis for it, then Growth, Understanding and Results will draw Gods people.

The book of Matthew has a variety of advantages for study. First, the Kingdom of God starts with Jesus' linage, through which He is born and established as the PROMISED ONE. Then John the Baptizer announces Jesus as the 'The Lamb of God who takes away the sin of the world. Jesus then establishes himself to do what God the FATHER sent him to do, by NOT yielding to the temptations placed before him by Satan. Jesus succeeds in remaining sinless and proves HE AS MAN is worthy to take back the title deed of the earth from Satan who stole it by deception from the 1ˢᵗ ADAM. From Matthew chapter 4:17 Jesus announces the KINGDOM OF HEAVEN IS AT HAND. I believe that this verse is interpreted in a somewhat misleading way. The idea given is that Jesus, as God, is establishing Gods' Kingdom on earth. When in reality, JESUS was establishing a basis for returning the title deed to earth TO MANKIND.

The idea which I began to develop from the revelation that Jesus was establishing a title deed transfer of the Earth back to man, new vistas of insight began to emerge. WHAT THIS REALLY MEANT TO ME WAS I SHOULD BE ABLE TO DO EXACTLY WHAT JESUS SAID I SHOULD BE DOING. The Kingdom of God is here right now and is here for the taking if we know how to inter into it.

Now, as I began to study the PARABLES and the HEALINGS in the book of Matthew and the other gospels, Mark, Luke and John, I began to see every—thing in a new way. I STARTED COMPARING HOW EACH GOSPEL COMPLIMENTED EACH OTHER from different reference points. In this regard; MATTHEW is written for the JEWS. MARK is written for the YOUNG MAN, LUKE is written for the INTELLECTUAL MAN And, JOHN is written for the COMMON MAN. It is interesting to note here, that many people look for the so called error of differences in the gospels instead of the enhancements they bring. Every word that God put in the Bible is significant and has significance for clarification and understanding. In addition, all of the other letters written to the CHURCHES written by the APPOSTALS AGREE WITH THE FOUR GOSPELS in as much as they totally support the FOUR GOSPELS.

When JESUS HEALED, I noticed that he never intruded upon a person's WILL, but always held back until invited into the situation. Another way of saying that Jesus was a gentleman and waited to be invited BEFORE he under took any healing action. Since Jesus is PERFECT THEOLOGY I determined to take my cue from Jesus and behave just as he did. I noticed right away that I began to get the same results that Jesus got when I employed the same way Jesus did it. This meant I had to be thoroughly familiar with each and every way Jesus healed. During this time in my life, it was the most exciting time I could have imagined.

As I studied the FOUR Gospels with HEALING AS MY FOCUS, I began to make Scriptural notations that revealed certain patterns that were alike OR different ways Jesus undertook to heal. IT was during this time that I put a brochure together on HOW TO BE HEALDED and began to share with those in the Church Classes which I was teaching. Most of the People received it well. Some did not.

CHAPTER 5

A LIFE-TIME OF STUDY AND EXPERIENCE KEY LESSONS FOR EVERYBODY

Every—one is not going to love you or even like you if you teach JESUS and are serious about following Him. ('If they heated me, they will hate you') (Matthew 10:22). This is what JESUS would happen, why are we surprised?

Some people will be resentful of you because you get the RESULTS the BIBLE says you SHOULD EXPECT. (Matthew 12: 2-8)

There are those who are curious about Jesus and simply want to know how to access His power without receiving Him. (Luke 10:49-50)

Not everyone is thank-full when they receive their healing from Jesus. (Ten Lepers) Luke 17:17

There are some blockages to healing. "This kind comes out by prayer and fasting" This is what Jesus said when his disciples came to him and said that they could not cast out a demon of a man. The question then follows. Why? It is therefore necessary to know what you are dealing with and if you are equipped to undertake the task. Jesus clarifies by introducing 'prayer and fasting'. This would indicate that prayer and fasting increases a person's Spiritual authority. Jesus then demonstrates this by casting the demon out of the man.

Another major obstacle for healing for a great many people is un-forgiveness of themselves and more importantly, of others. One of the major points of un-forgiveness is the the effect it has on the person who holds un-forgiveness. I have observed that severe sicknesses illness and disease come upon that person and they don't know why. The opposite of LOVE IS UN-FORGIVENESS. out of un-forgiveness comes many ills. Out of LOVE, flow many blessings, to the forgiving person first and then to those that are connected to that person.

The Bible says that every knee shall bend to the name of Jesus and every tongue shall confess that Jesus is Lord. (On Earth and in Heaven) Then again it says that every name shall bow at the name of Jesus. This started me to think about how God has set up His Kingdom in one specific way. First, It dawned on me that everything on Earth and every—thing in Heaven has *a name.* This was highly interesting to me. Second, every name carries authority. Finally, the name that carries the most authority is *The Name of Jesus.* Now, the next part I am about to write is not speculation but revealed knowledge. The Holy Spirit revealed to me that we as Christians must know the names of our friends as well as our adversaries if we are to function properly in a sin/sick World. Since our adversary has authority and God has greater authority, we must learn how to access that greater authority in both the natural world and the spirit world. You might ask how do you know that it was the HOLY SPIRIT revealing this to you? Because the Bible says it is the assigned role of the Holy Spirit to lead us into *all* Truth. The Bible also says that the Truth shall make you free.

UNFORGIVENESS AND BITTERNESS

Jesus knew that un-forgiveness and bitterness would be a hindrance to his love for the very people He came to save. Jesus had to SPEAK FORGIVENESS FROM THE CROSS. 'Father, forgive them, for they know not what they do' It was these words of Jesus from the cross that erased all residue of sin that could hinder Jesus from completing his Earthly ministry as a 'Son of Man'.

Many times in our lives we feel that life has thrown un-fair circumstances our way, and we may feel that God has abandoned us to the difficulty we face. For me, these are the times I stop and take a real close look at what Jesus went through for me. I take Communion, follow the Biblical command of Jesus himself and simply remember what he did for me as I take each element, The Bread and the Wine, each in turn. The bread first, which was his body broken for me. Then the wine, which was his blood, shed for me. During these times, I can't help but think of the masterful job Mel Gibson did in, the movie depiction of 'The Passion of Christ'.

Each time I enter into a communion time with Jesus by the breaking of the bread and the taking of the wine, I have the same physical reaction. I have new surge of energy, strength and life. (a great sense of peace and well-being always follows). I remember the very detail of Jesus' suffering for me in the following ways:

1). Jesus in the garden of Gethsemane sweat great drops of blood. (His blood—shed for me).

2). Jesus brought before the Council of the Sanhedrin and beaten and bloodied and his beard pulled out of his face. (His blood—shed for me).

3). Jesus handed over to Pilot for whipping in preparation for death on the cross. Jesus took 39 lashings on his back and front. (His blood—shed for me) (It just so happens that there are 39 categories of human diseases) 'By his stripes we are healed' (Isaiah 53:5) we confirm it, by speaking it out loud.

4). Jesus had a crown of thorns pressed into his head. (His blood—shed for me).

5). Jesus fainted on the road to Calvary from the lack of blood in his body and had to be helped by Simon, a man from Cyrene, whom they compelled to carry his Jesus' cross (His blood—shed for me)

6). Jesus at Calvary had his hands individually and separately nailed to the cross. (His blood—shed for me)

7). Jesus' feet were crossed over and nailed together to the cross. (His blood—shed for me).

Jesus is ridiculed, taunted, insulted and challenged to come down from the cross if he is the Son of God. Had Jesus done so then WE would still be in our sin, hopeless and helpless. Jesus hung there three hours and died having made a concluding statement 'IT IS FINISHED'.

'IT IS FINISHED MEANS—WE ARE RESTORED TO OUR ORIGINAL GOD INTENDED POSITION ON EARTH, NOTHING MISSING, NOTHING BROKEN. I CAN NOW EXERSIZE MY WORD AUTHORITY AS DID THE FIRST ADAM AND LAST ADAM JESUS. MY LIFE AND HEALTH ARE RENEWED MY SALVATION IS ASSURED. *TO ALL OF THIS I SAY ALLELUYAH; SALVATION, AND GLORY AND HONOR, AND POWER, UNTO THE LORD OUR GOD—AMEN AND AMEN*

At this point, I will go back to our major building block of the 'Kingdom of God', which is the Spoken Word. When used in the proper way, words are our most useful provision from God. However, when improperly used, words are our worst enemy. One excellent Scriptural example is a passage in Matthew 12: 34. Jesus speaks to the Scribes and Pharisees in this manner, "O generation of vipers, how can you, being evil, speak good things? For out of the abundance of the heart the mouth speaks." Then Jesus compares, "A good man out of the good treasure of the heart brings forth good things. But, *I say unto you, that every idle word that men shall speak, they shall give account thereof in the day of Judgment. For by your words thou shall be justified, and by your words you shall be condemned." Matthew 12: 35-37.*

Other Scripture expands the authority of Speaking and gives us an understanding of the effect our speech has on our lives. *Proverbs 15: 1 'A soft answer turns away wrath: but grievous words stir up anger. Proverbs 15: 2 The tongue of the wise uses knowledge rightly; but the mouth of fools pour out foolishness. Proverbs 15; 7 The lips of the wise disperse knowledge: but the heart of the foolish doeth not so. Proverbs 17: 9 He that covers a transgression seeks love; but he that repeats a matter separates true friends. Proverbs 17: 4 A wicked doer gives heed to false lips; and a liar gives ear to a naughty tongue. Proverbs: 17: 27 He that has knowledge spares his words; and a man of understanding is of an excellent spirit. Proverbs 18: 7 A fools mouth is his destruction, and his lips are the snare of his soul.*

To sum it all up

Proverbs 20: 20-21 'A man's belly shall be satisfied with the fruit of his mouth and with the increase of his lips shall he be filled. Death and life are in the power of the tongue; and they that love it shall eat the fruit thereof.

May the Lord give us complete understanding of the smallest member of our head, the tongue. If we are to grow and prosper in the KINGDOM OF GOD, we must learn to master the tongue or Sin may lay at the door and come in.

In the book of *Mark* 11: 12, there are two intertwining story-lines. One is concerned with a fig tree that has leaves and no fruit and *Mark* 11: 24 in which Jesus instructs His disciples concerning when they pray, and the effect that an unforgiving attitude has on God's answer to our prayer. First, in looking at the fig tree which has leaves but no fruit, if you have ever owned or observed a fig tree and the way It produces fruit, you know that the small tender figs always appear on the fig tree before any leaves ever appear. So when Jesus saw a fig tree that has leaves on it, his expectation was that *the fig tree should also have figs.* Since the fig tree has leaves and no fruit, Jesus curses the tree at the root. (Some of you may not have heard this before, but, Israel is represented by two trees in the Bible. One tree is the Fig Tree *represents Religious Israel.* The other tree is the *Olive Tree, which represents National Israel.)*

The significance of the Fig Tree is that as Jesus was entering Jerusalem to address the religious leaders who were supposed to have the *fruit of the Word of the Old Testament he finds that their words are empty and without fruit.* Jesus condemns the works of the religious leaders and tells them that *their house is left desolate.* The symbol is clearly identified with Jesus cursing the fig tree because it has no fruit, and the Jewish Temple which would soon be destroyed by the Romans 70ad.

In the Mark 11:24 passage, Jesus is telling his disciples that whenever they pray, whatever they say must carry with it the conviction that it will come about just as it is spoken if they believe it. In verse 25 of Mark 11, Jesus makes a very important point that allows God to hear and answer your prayer without interference of un-forgiveness in your heart. We *must forgive if we want God to answer our prayers.*

The real issue in both of these Scriptures is,that whatever the outside appearance, God requires truth in our works and that which is done for Him. In addition, we may even be blocking our own blessing if we are not re-examining our motives in light what Jesus has done for us. Some Traditions in the Church can cause us to believe that we are on the right path in following Jesus when all we are doing is *what is comfortable.*

What Ever You Start—Finish

As a child growing up, I learned, what-ever you start, finish it. In addition, before you start, count the cost. If you start, don't turn back. Finally, finish strong. These have been the hallmarks of my life.

At twelve years old, I made a decision to follow Jesus. I counted the cost, I decided I was not going to turn back and I would finish strong. Throughout my 72 years of life I have tried to live by this creed. Today, I feel more strongly about my decision to follow Jesus than ever before. This is as it should be. This does not mean it will be easy. Whatever is easy is not worth the struggle. Often, events did not allow for whatever we commit ourselves to be completely in our control. After all, we are in the world with people who also have a free-will. From this I learned, how to work with people, but, I never ever gave up my principles of following Jesus, counting the cost, not turning back and finishing strong.

During my childhood, I became quite competitive with my peers in a quiet kind of way. I would look for ways to innovate and try things others did not think of. My attitude was mainly formed by the fact that in the latter part of March in 1950, I contracted Polio. According to our family Doctor, I had polio a disease which paralyzes the lungs over time. As it turns out, when I was in a sleep state, I had an encounter with the Spirit World. My impression was, I encountered an angel. This angelic—being informed me that I was going to be sent back to the place I came from because it was not my time yet. Almost immediately, I was in a bed at home which I did not remember getting in too. I felt perfectly well and not stiff at all, and, I could function perfectly. My mother was in the kitchen cooking and I could smell something really good and I got really hungry. I got out of the bed and went into the kitchen. When my mother saw me, I could tell that she thought that I was not supposed to be able to do that. She called the Doctor who came over immediately and pronounced that a miracle must have happened because he had no explanation for my recovery. That was confirmation to me that God was real and that I was valuable to Him.

From that moment on, I was absolutely sure that there was an angel watching over me. It was later that I understood that Jesus had to have angels minister to him. Remember Jesus, when he fasted in the wilderness forty (40) days? The Book of Mark, Chapter 1:13 it states; 'and he (Jesus) was in the wilderness forty days, tempted of Satan; and was with the wild beasts; and the angels ministered unto him.' This scripture, taken together with other confirming scripture, that Jesus, when He left Heaven to take on flesh and become 'son of man', he Jesus, had to finish what he started as man and his mission had to be completed as a man. Satan evidently understood this also because he asked the question in the passage of Luke, Chapter 4:3 when he said to Jesus 'and the devil said to him *if thou be the SON of GOD, command this stone to be made bread. JESUS ANSWERED him, saying, IT IS WRITTEN, THAT MAN SHALL NOT LIVE BY BREAD ALONE BUT BY EVERY WORD THAT PROCEDS FROM THE MOUTH OF GOD.*

If Satan had succeeded in getting Jesus to turning the stone into bread AS SON of GOD, then Jesus would have failed in the redemption of Man. The reason is clear, If Jesus had turned the stone into bread as the SON of GOD then GOD would be made a liar, because GOD said in Genesis 1:26, 'and GOD said, LET US MAKE MAN IN OUR IMAGE, AFTER OUR LIKENESS: AND LET THEM HAVE DOMINION OVER THE FISH OF THE SEA, AND OVER THE FOWL OF THE AIR, AND OVER THE CATTLE, AND OVER EVERY CREEPING THING THAT CREEPTH UPON THE EARTH.

It is thus made clear that MAN must act in the same way that Jesus acted while on Earth as a MAN. Jesus always deferred to the OLD TESTAMENT scripture as his authority in every—thing he did and said. As NEW TESTAMENT PEOPLE, we must learn the provisions, understand and act on what we are given as a result of what Jesus did in establishing us as His disciples. AS WE LEARN THE PROVISIONS AVAILABLE TO US, WE WILL BE WELL ABLE TO DO WHAT JESUS INSTRUCTED US TO DO. *WHAT WE STARTED WHEN WE ACCEPTED JESUS INTO OUR HEARTS, WE WILL ALSO COMPLETE AND FINISH STRONG. IF WE FOLLOW THE EXAMPLE OF JESUS IN EVERY DETAIL, WE WILL BE SUCCESSFUL.*

WHEN WE LOOK BEYOND THE BIG LIE

Mankind is constantly attacked by *IDEAS, THOUGHTS and SUGGESTIONS.* Those negative ideas, thoughts and suggestions that come to us by sudden intrusion and without warning, can be traced back to our enemy, Satan. Since the enemy does not want us to know He exists. *He always attempts to deceive us by making us think that all thoughts come from ourselves. As demonstrated earlier, this is not true.* (Satan is referred to as the Prince of the airways) In common terms this means that Satan has access to our minds by His *THOUGHTS, IDEAS and SUGGESTIONS.*

One of the main points of attack SATAN FINDS IN MANKIND IS OUR UNBELIEF IN WHAT GOD HAS SPOKEN OR GIVEN TO MAN TO WRITE DOWN AND PASS ON. Satan does this by planting in our minds that somehow God is unfair and is the CAUSE of all things. This leads to the idea that God is responsible for everything that happens. THEREFORE the phrase, 'GOD IS IN CONTROL'. THEREFORE GODS' WILL IS INVOLVED IN EVERY THING THAT HAPPENS TO US. Now, Satan has the opportunity to plant in our minds that anything that happens to us is from God and IT IS GOD'S WILL. *SO WE SUFFER THROUGH IT THINKING THAT GOD BROUGHT IT ALL TO US.* THAT IS THE BIG LIE WHICH WE NEED TO GET BEYOND AND SEE THE TRUTH FOR WHAT IS STATED IN THE *BIBLE.* GOD IS GOOD AND ADDS NO SORROW.

'The Lord is my Sheppard I shall not want, He makes me to lay down in green pastures, he leads me beside still waters, he restores my soul, he leads me in paths of righteousness for his names' sake. Yes though I walk through the valley of the shadow of death, I will fear no evil, Thy rod and thy staff they comfort me. Thou prepare a table before me in the present of my enemies, thou anoint my head with oil, my cup runs over. Surely goodness and mercy shall follow me all the days of my life, and, I shall dwell in the house of the Lord forever.

If we look beyond the BIG LIE, we will not fail. God is good and he is always good. Keep your faith and finish strong. Know your God and never give up. The reward is greater than the cost.

WHAT TO LOOK FOR

Men and women, because we live in a material world, we rely heavily on our senses, we tend to see every—thing through that exposure. Since Satan lives in the spirit world, we don't get to see him in his normal state of being. This fact gives him the opportunity to deceive us by his ability to cloak himself in disguise which is designed to trick us in to a mind—set that says that he is not as bad as we have been told. And, because what we are told as we grew up is that Satan, as the devil is really to be feared and avoided at all costs, we now have a problem. The problem is that our senses, of which we rely so heavily, is the gateway that opens the door to the Satan's world. NOW, SINCE OUR SENSES ARE THE GATE WAY TO OUR EXPERIENCE WITH THE WORLD, AND SATAN CONTROLS THE WORLD SYSTEMS, HE CAN MANIPULATE OUR INVIORNMENT SO THAT WE ARE SUBJECT TO THE SENSE WORLD AND NOT THE SPIRIT WORLD. HIS APPEAL IS ALWAYS TO OUR FLESH AND NOT OUR SPIRIT. We see this at the very beginning in Genesis 3:1-14. Go back and read these verses very carefully. And you will see the deceptive words Satan uses to deceive the woman. Satan's appeal was to the woman's senses.

Some—what later, Adam, the man was involved with his decision to test his senses also. The Bible says, 'And when the woman *saw* that the tree was good for *food, and that it was pleasant to the eyes,* and a tree desired to make *one wise, She took of the fruit thereof, and did eat,* and gave also to unto *husband with her* and *he did eat.' Genesis 3:6.* Now they are both without excuse and will both be accountable for what they were told. GOD starts with the instigator, Satan. God separates the seed of the devil from, the woman's *seed*. (The woman's seed is separated from Satan's *seed* (1/3 of the Angels that followed Satan). God then states, '*The seed of the woman shall crush Satan's* head.' The seed of the woman, (Mary) would bring forth JESUS to crush the serpent's head on Calvary, on a lonely cross, to die for all mankind, and restore that which was lost by the man and the woman (Adam) disobeying God. Satan is assigned to eating dust and going on his belly from that time forward, and in addition, having his head crushed in the future. (His power taken away)

The BIG LIE often entails long held Biblical interpretations of Gods intents without reconciling them with the Word. JESUS says to His disciples in 'Matthews 10: 5-8'

'Go not in the way of the Gentiles, and to any city of the Samaritans enter ye not. But go rather to the lost sheep of the house of Israel. And as you go, preach, saying, the kingdom of heaven is at hand. Heal the sick, cleanse the lepers, raise the dead, cast out devils, freely you have received, freely give'.

Now any one reading this verse in context to the entire chapter of Matt.10:1-42 would know that Jesus is sending his disciples on a training mission so that they will be equipped for the WORK after HE was crucified. The disciples were to practice their WORK on the LOST SHEEP of ISRAEL, the very ones JESUS came to SAVE. This fact however, does not preclude the principle of healing for the people of the Church to day. In fact the blueprint for the way the Church should be moving today is the entire Book of Matthew. The Church is the heir of the Kingdom of God by way of being graphed into the heritage of Israel as Abrahams' seed by way of the Wild Olive Tree. Matthew demonstrates perfectly all of the operational principles of the Kingdom of God.

The FIRST principle is that the kingdom of God works on KNOWLEDGE. 'Matthew 9:35' 'And JESUS went about *all the cities and villages, TEACHING in their synagogues, and Preaching the Gospel of the Kingdom, and Healing every Sickness and every Disease among the People'*. 'Matthew 9:36' says, the SECOND principle is UNDERSTANDING. 'But when he saw the multitudes, he was moved with compassion on them, because they fainted and were scattered abroad, as sheep having no shepherd'. The Shepherd comes along side the sheep and guides them into green pastures. Where they will not faint, but be refreshed by UNDERSTANDING. The THRID principle is WISDOM. Matthew 9: 37-38 says, 'Then said he unto his disciples, 'The harvest truly is plenteous, but the labors are few; Pray ye therefore the LORD of the

HEARVEST, that he will send forth laborers in to the harvest'. The clear operational principle is that Wisdom is the place where we put wisdom in action, and actually do the Work God says to do without fear of failure. I believe this is a principle applicable to the Church today when we are equipped properly in these Three Principles: KNOWLEDGE, UNDERSTANDING, and WISDOM.

To further make the point CLEAR, 'Matthew 10: 1 states, And when he called unto him his twelve disciples, he gave them power against unclean spirits, to cast them out, and to heal all manner of sickness and all manner of disease. The next verse brings a list of the twelve Apostles sent out to do the WORK. Simon called Peter, his brother Andrew, James and John the sons of Zebedee, Philip, and Bartholomew, Thomas and Matthew the publican, James the son of Alphaeus, and Lebbeaus whose surname was Thaddaeus, Simon the Canaanite and *Judas Iscariot*, who betrayed him. These twelve Jesus sent forth,' Now It puzzled me for some time, why did Judas Iscariot go and do the WORK with the HOLY SPIRIT, yet fail to stay in and remain with the Twelve? It was not until I realized that Jesus only empowered them to do the WORK. But that the HOLY SPIRIT WAS NOT GIVEN TO LIVE IN MAN UNTIL FIFTY (50) DAYS AFTER JESUS ROSE FROM THE DEAD ON THE DAY OF PENTACOST IN THE UPPER ROOM.

Even though Judas carried the Purse for the Apostles, he was subject to his own greed and sold Jesus for thirty pieces of silver. It then follows that by betraying Jesus to the Chief Priest Judas was hoping that Jesus would be forced to show himself as the Messiah and establish the Kingdom with Judas as the TREASURER. IT did not work and Judas is now left holding the bag. Realizing his error, he tries to give back the thirty (30) pieces of silver. The priests refuse and Judas throws the money at them and in a hopeless state of mind goes out and hangs himself.

The life and outcome of the of Judas Iscariots' life should act as a reminder of those things that draw us away from Jesus and we lose sight of the bigger picture of our Salvation and the WORK WITH WHICH WE ARE ENGAGED.

What we must constantly be on guard against falling in to the trap of Knowledge only. But, we must be constantly on guard and looking for ways of entering into Understanding for the salvation of man-kind. First, starting with the Church, we must learn to blend Understanding with Knowledge so that Wisdom can shine through in the form of Results. As we do the Work of

God, Results are Signs that draws the world into the knowledge of God. If you are sick, you want to be healed. If you are broken you want to be made whole. If you are down, you want to be lifted up. The Church is the place where these things are designed to take place if we follow the mandate of Jesus. 'Go into all the world and preach the Gospel to every creature. He that believes and is baptized shall be saved; but he that believes not shall be damned. And these signs shall follow them that believe; *In my name shall they cast out devils; they speak with new tongues; They shall take up serpents; and if they drink any deadly thing, it shall not hurt them; they shall lay hands on the sick and they shall recover.* '(Mark 16:15-18)

'So then after the LORD had spoken unto them, he was received up into heaven, and sat on the right hand of God. And *they went forth, and the preached every where, the LORD working with them and confirming the WORD with signs following.* Amen.' (Mark 16:19-20)

It is time for the Church to move out of its' comfort zone, walking the streets, putting stakes in the ground to stake out your territory for victory in physical ways, visible ways and verbal ways. Preach the gospel where ever you go. Don't worry about the result. God will work with you and signs will follow you where ever you go. This has been my experience and I am no different than you.

Since God has put a calling on my life to TEACH THE WORD and THE SIGNS have followed me, I am FIRMLY CONVIENCED that GOD never changes and is not a respecter of persons. HE will use anyone who is willing to be used. Do not be afraid. Be strong and courageous. Chart your course, make provision for your journey, set your time to move out, move out on the power of the Word and watch the way God will WORK WITH YOU. Amen.

CHAPTER 6

ANGELS WILL HELP US

In order to achieve anything in this life or in your Spiritual life, there are two words you must keep in mind. They are to be, *fully persuaded.* One cannot half step into the Kingdom of God. One must take a full step of faith or don't step at all. Any worth—while endeavor requires a full commitment if we are to succeed in that endeavor. Satan tries to frighten us into being timid in a false humility. He plants thoughts like, 'Who do you think you are? What makes you think you can do that'? After all, that healing stuff went out with the Apostles. You are told many things that follow after the traditions of men, most of which will not stand up to close examination. In order to be *fully persuaded*, you must be willing to examine closely whatever you are told, and, most assuredly the things in the Bible. Let us take a close look at some of the biblical elements that make us confident and not fear.

ANGELS There are not only Gods' angels, but there are fallen angels—angels that rebelled against God. It is good to know about what the Bible says about fallen angels. One third of the angels in heaven followed Lucifer when he rebelled against GOD. As a result, they lost their first estate (place) in GODS' heaven. (Rev. 12:9.) Also, let us look at (JUDE 1:6)

And the angels which kept not their first estate, but left their own habitation, he hath reserved in everlasting chains under darkness unto the judgment of the great day.

Notice these angels are reserved in everlasting chains under darkness. Now, take a look at (2Peter 2:4-5). He states the angels' kept not their first estate.' They sinned, and lost their habitation. The Hebrew says 'they kept not their first headship or dominion.'

For GOD spared not the angels that sinned, but cast them down to hell, and delivered them into chains of darkness, to be reserved unto judgment; And spared not the old world, but saved NOAH the eight person, a preacher of Righteousness, bringing in the flood upon the world of the ungodly.

Looking carefully at this passage, we find that Lucifer was a leader of the angels in GODS' first creative order before Man was created. Let us look at another passage which confirms this. (Ezekiel 28:12-15)

Son of Man, take up a lamentation upon the king of Tyrus, and say unto him, Thus said the LORD GOD; Thou sealeth up the sum, full of wisdom, and perfect in beauty. THOU HAST BEEN IN EDEN THE GARDEN OF GOD; Every precious stone was thy covering, the sardius, topaz, and the diamond, the beryl, the onyx and the jasper, the sapphire, the emerald,and the carbuncle, and the gold workmanship of thy tabrets and of thy pipes was prepared to thee in the day that thou was created. Thou art the anointed cherub that covers; and I have set thee so: thou was upon the holy mountain of GOD; thou hast walked up and down in the midist of the stones of fire, Thou was perfect in thy ways from the day that thou was created, till iniquity was found in thee.

In this passage, GOD refers to Lucifer as the anointed cherub which designates high authority and position and access to GOD unimpeded.

Take note, The Garden of God does *not* mean the Garden of Eden, they are two different places. The garden of God was in Heaven and the garden of Eden was on the Earth.

Lucifer had access to GODS' Garden in heaven before he fell and took one—third of the angels with him. Before Lucifer fell, he had all kinds of precious jewels and gold as his covering. After his fall, that was taken away. We know this because in the Garden of Eden (the garden of Adam) Lucifer appeared as a serpent and he was wearing a snake skin, not decked out in jewels and gold.

After man was created, Lucifer sees an opportunity to get back some of what he lost when God stripped him of his kingdom in the heavens.

By disobedience, Adam the man and the woman lose their dominion over the Earth. Nevertheless, GOD had a plan to restore what Lucifer disrupted. Lucifer's plan involved sending his fallen angels to the earth to corrupt the seed of the woman so that the seed of the woman could not bring forth *the one* who would deliver mankind from an eternity of sin, sickness and death. Gods' plan works to a limited degree and God has to take all corruption away by a World—wide flood. His plan also involves a man called Abram who was to be renamed Abraham from the land called UR. (Today called Iraq) Out of which comes the Hebrew Nations and in particular a Tribe called JUDAH from which comes *JESUS* the promised one.

It is only natural that Lucifer would want his former position back, but to persist in a fixation on sitting in the seat of God? This takes Lucifer beyond repair and puts him in the category of rebellion against the HOLY GOD. Now Isaiah12:17 reads:

How art thou fallen from heaven, Oh Lucifer, son of the morning! How are thou cut down to the ground, which did weaken the nations! For thou hast said in thy heart, I will exault (lift) my thrown above the stars of GOD. I will sit also upon the Mount of the congregation, in the sides of the north: I will ascend above the heights of the clouds; I will be like the most HIGH. Yet thou shall be brought down to hell, to the sides of the Pit.

A careful reading of the last sentence, '*Yet thou shall be brought down to hell, to the sides of the Pit.*' tells us that GOD intends to judge Lucifer in the future for his rebellion against GOD. It is interesting to note that all the fallen angels will be judged in the future.

ANGELIC DOMINION

For Christ also hath once suffered for sins, the just for the unjust, that he might bring us to GOD, being put to death in the flesh, but quickened by the Spirit:

By which also he went and preached unto the spirits in prison;

Which sometime were disobedient, when once the longsuffering of GOD waited in the days of Noah, while the ark was a preparing, wherein few, that is, eight souls were saved by water. (1 Peter 3: 18-20)

It was hard for me to understand when I was a new Christian exactly what this passage meant. However, as I read more and started to put things together, I discovered that JESUS DID A MULTITUDE OF THINGS AT THE TIME OF HIS DEATH, BURIAL AND RESURRECTION. HERE ARE SOME THAT COME TO THE FOREFRONT;

1) The penalty for sin is paid for
2) Hades can no longer hold the Righteous
3) Jesus' name is the only name by which we must be saved
4) Jesus paid the penalty for all sickness, illness and disease.

5) Jesus has a Name above all names
6) Heaven and Earth are cleansed of sin
7) Angels and spirits are told the new order of authority
8) Mans dominion is restored
9) All Christians are joint heirs to all of GODS' promises under the new Covenant

   When Jesus preached to the 'spirits in prison' He was preaching to the fallen angels and their offspring, the giants of Noah's day, who no longer have a body, but, are spirits in the under-world.

Jesus is evidently giving the Spirits in hell a list of the things they must obey now that He has paid the penalty for all of the past, present and future sins of man. 'Therefore there is no more condemnation for sin'.

Hebrews 1:7 states "And of the angels he says, who makes his angels spirits, and his ministers a flame of fire". *HE MAKES HIS ANGELS SPIRITS.*

Angels were created before man in a world we are told little about. Lucifer existed in a world before Adam. When Lucifer came to the Garden of Eden, he was already a fallen being. He had lost his throne. When he appeared on this earth he had already lost his dominion. He was not covered with jewels or precious stone, he had lost it all in the fall. He came to Earth to deceive man and gain control over the earth and take authority. He did what he came to do. ADAM SOLD HIS EARTH LEASE IN EXCHANGE FOR THE KNOWLEDGE OF GOOD AND EVIL.

There is a lease on Earth that is a six thousand years lease given to man.

When the lease runs out, Satan knows he has had it, and there is no more time to make his case before GOD, and justify his rebellion, using man as his excuse.

Satan knows his time is getting short and the demons know it also. An example in(Matthew 8:28-32) we find that Jesus has just crossed the Sea of Galilee into the country of the Gaderenes. He and his disciples are met by two demon filled possessed men. Recognizing Jesus as the Son of God, they plead for Jesus to *not* send them to the place of torment (The PIT) they ask to be sent into a herd of pigs. Jesus accommodates them and when the pigs were possessed, they ran down a cliff and killed them—selves. The amazing thing is that the demon possessed said to Jesus '*have you come to torment us before the time.* (Mark 5:7) puts it this way, they said 'I adjure you by GOD that you torment us not'. *This is even more amazing, the demons are invoking the name of GOD to Jesus to be fair and don't send us back to the Pit before our time is up.* The demons know more than most Christians. Don't you think we should know at least what the demons know?

Josephus, the Jewish historian, made this statement: "Many angels of God accompanied (women) and begat sons that proved unjust." (You will notice that the angels begat sons and no mention of angels having daughters). The sons mentioned here are the giants of old and a part of Lucifer plan to mess up the gene pool of mankind.

Then in Isaiah 26:13, 14, there is an interesting note. In doing a study on the word *giants,* you find the word 'Raphaims has been used in the Scripture for *giants* the word means "dead," It refers to *the dead that will not be raised!* The giant race will not be raised up again. God has destroyed them physically (by the 'Flood') but not their spirit. They will not have a future resurrection for judgment as likewise the fallen angels will not have a resurrection. However, they will both be judged. What we see today, with respect to the dead giants killed by the world-wide flood, is the spirits of the dead giants who are invited up to the surface of the earth by voodoo, witch-craft, and other occult practices. It is also interesting to note that the spirits of the giants can—not come to the earth surface on their own, they must be invited up by mankind. This the legal requirement God set-up in Genesis by establishing man as dominion on the Earth.

Giants stole the dominion from mankind by the fact that their sheer size and strength could not be easily opposed and the fallen angels assisted them in enslaving mankind. When a spirit is invited up to the surface of the Earth by mankind and *enters a man* we call that *demon possession.* You will notice that demon possessed people are usually strong beyond their size. This strength comes from the memory of the demon spirit when *he had a giant body.* Jesus cast out demons in the course of His healing ministry. Since Jesus is our model and example for all of our behavior, we should pay close attention to, what did Jesus say? What did Jesus do? How did Jesus react to each of his life situations? Especially when we are engaged with the demonic world we must have a firm grip on what we have learned from the examples of JESUS.

The Bible says, 'that when a spirit is cast out of a person, he wonders in dry places, (deserts) seeking a place (person) to occupy'. Finding none, he returns to the man/woman he came out of and finds it swept and clean, (but not occupied by *the Holy Spirit)*, he then goes and finds seven more spirits even more wicked than himself and they go and occupy that man. Then *that man is worse off than at the first.*

The clear emphasis here is that, we as Christians must be taught more about what the Bible says about Angels and demons, their origins, their purpose and their intents towards man-kind. Now let's take a look at JESUS and the angels.

JESUS AND THE ANGELS

As we look at this, we will take a look at Hebrews 1:1-14 in order to establish a scriptural foundation for understanding JESUS and the ANGELS.

God, who at sundry times and in divers manners spoke in time past unto the fathers by the prophets, v.1

Has in these last days spoken unto us by his SON,whom he has appointed heir to all things, by whom also he made the worlds :v.2

Who being the the brightness of his glory, and the express image of his person, and up holding all things by the word of his power, when he had by himself purged our sins, sat down on the right hand of the majesty on high; v.3

Being made so much better than the angels, as he hath by inheritance obtained a more excellent name than they, v.4

For unto which of the angels said he at any time, 'Thou are my Son, this day have I begotten thee? And again, I will be to him a Father, and he shall be to me a Son? v.5

And again, when he brings in the first-begotten into the world, he said, And let all the angels of God worship him.v.6

And of the angels he said, Who makes his angels SPIRITS and HIS MINISTERS, a FLAME OF FIRE.v.7

But unto the Son he says, thy throne, O God, is for—ever and ever; a scepter of righteousness is the scepter of thy KINGDOM. v.8

And, Thou loved righteousness, and hated iniquity; therefore God, even thy God, has anointed thee with the oil of gladness above thy fellows. v.9

And, Thou, Lord, in the beginning has laid the foundation of the earth; and the heavens are the works of thy hands; they shall perish; but thou remain; and they all shall wax old as doth a garment; v.10

And as a vesture, shall thou fold them up, and they shall be changed; but thou are the same, and thy years shall not fail. v. 12-11

But to which of the angels says he at any time, Sit on my right hand, until I make your enemies your footstool? v.13

Are they not all ministering Spirits, sent forth to minister for them who shall be heirs of salvation. v.14

Once JESUS' identity is established, then the writer of Hebrews compares Him to angels. 'He being made so much better than the angels, as he hath by inheritance obtained a more excellent name than they.' Hebrew 1; 4

JESUS IS GREATER THAN All THE ANGELS GREATER IN POWER AND AUTHORITY

He has obtained His position by inheritance, by conquest and it was bestowed upon Him. Because of his obedience, Jesus has been given *THE PLACE OF PREEMINENCE ON THE RIGHT HAND OF GOD.* The angels, however, are our servants. They are ministering sprits sent to minister for the heirs of salvation.

Ask yourself: WHO ARE THE HEIRS OF SALVATION?

The heirs are: **EVERY JESUS CONFESSING—BIBLE BELIEVING—JESUS FOLLOWER.**

Just as Jesus had to learn how to accomplish the provisions GOD laid out for him to give us the Salvation we enjoy, he also had to learn how to walk in the SPIRIT so he would not fulfill the lusts of the flesh. Each of the the three things that make us heirs to Salvation, show us action words. Confession, Believing and Following also show us a process that is moving forward. That is, heirs of Salvation are always in motion to do what is needed in accomplishing the Work of the Kingdom of GOD.

The Bible says, 'every knee will bow, every tongue confess that JESUS CHRIST is LORD'. The difference between bowing the knee voluntarily and confessing that Jesus is Lord voluntarily, is the difference between being a legitimate heir and a illegitimate pretender. All of creation will be subject to bowing the knee.

HOW ARE WE CONNECTED TO ANGELS

When take a look at our relationship to Angels, we must first look at the relationship that Jesus had to the Angels. According to the Bible in the Book of John, 'Jesus as the WORD, created all things by the power of His WORD.' Since Jesus is our Perfect Theology, this means that if Jesus had a relationship with the Angels as Creator then we also have a relationship with the Angels as a part of the Creative Order.

Jesus' birth was announced by Angels, his young life was protected by angels when Joseph and Mary were warned to flee to Egypt to avoid Herod killing the infants two and under. After Jesus was Thirty years old, he was driven into the wilderness after he was baptized by John the Baptist in the Jordon River. At the end of the forty days and forty nights in the wilderness, Angels were sent to minister to him after he fasted and was tempted of the Devil. Again Jesus was tempted in the Garden as he prayed that God remove the cup of suffering He was about to face and an Angel came and ministered to Jesus after he decided to go to the cross.

Since Jesus had Angels that ministered to him in all these examples, it seems to me that Jesus would make no less a provision for those He called to be Saints. I believe that we are all in the same place of protection that Jesus was in, with the Angels ministering to Him. Many Old Testament Saints were afforded the same protection that Jesus was given. An Angel was sent to Daniel, by God to accomplish His work in letting Daniel know what the future would hold for the World through Daniel. In the example of the companions of Daniel, Shadrach, Meshach and Abednego, when they were walking in the fire, an angel was seen with them.

These examples make the point that Angles are a part of Gods' plan to assist man in this life and are a part of the provision made for man.

Psalm 91:8-12, 14, puts it this way . . . . Only with thin eyes shall thou behold and see the reward of the wicked.

Because thou has made the Lord, which is my refuge, even the the most High, thy habitation: there shall no evil befall the, neither shall any plague come nigh thy dwelling.

For he shall give his Angeles charge over you, to keep you in all your ways.

They shall bear thee up in their hands, lest thou dash thy foot against a stone.

Because he has set his love upon me, therefore will I deliver him: I will set him on high, because he has known my Name.

Psalm 91:15, 16, adds a further clarification . . . . He shall call upon me, and I will answer him: I will be with him in trouble; *I will deliver him, and I will honor him.*

With long life will I satisfy him, and show him my *salvation.*

The word salvation is defined as *"preservation, healing, soundness and deliverance from temporal evils",* according to Romans 10:9 and Hebrews 2:3.

How shall we escape if we neglect the deliverance that comes by the Ministry of Angles.

The ministry of angles is part of the salvation that God has provided for you. It's foolish to partake of *part of it* (salvation) and *not take part in all of it* (healing).

It is sad to say but, many Christians believe Jesus for their Salvation, but on the other hand these same Christians will not believe Jesus for their healing. These Christians say things like, 'I believe Jesus can heal me but that's in Gods hands'.

Or, statements like 'God will do it in His time and in the mean time, I believe

God is trying to *teach me something by this illness.* These type statements reveal that most Christians are taught out of the Old Testament and identify with the rebellion of ISRAEL. Therefore, they have put themselves in the position of punishment by God just as ISRAEL did. They have not made the transition to the New Testament provisions.

The Old Testament for the nation of Israel is a book of promises. The New Testament for the Christian is a book fulfilled promises. This is why we sing the song 'JESUS PAID IT ALL, ALL TO HIM I OWE, SIN HAD LEFT A CRIMSOME STAIN, HE WASHED IT ALL AWAY.' On the one hand, the Jews are still waiting for the promises of God, and, on the other hand God sent His Son Jesus and fulfill the promises with HIS PROVISIONS IN THE NEW TESTAMENT.

Peter 1:3 says it this way . . . . 'He has given us all things that pertain unto life and godliness.' All means all, and Salvation has THREE PARTS TO IT.

1)   Salvation . . . . Saved from Sin. and Destruction
2)   Restored . . . . Returned to the Original State
3)   Authority . . . . Renewed with power

Salvation conveys a lack of fear and doubt . . . . Restored conveys health returned. Authority . . . . conveys power in your words

How does God do these things as a practical matter, and, what is in play when we see the works of God manifest in the world.

God works in the natural, by this I mean that He shows himself in natural ways. What is more natural than your health? Your HEALTH is where you LIVE. With-in the Word Health is the word, 'Heal'. Heal is defined as: restored, or returned to the original natural state. This should not be more evident than in the Body of Christ, the CHURCH. As one of Gods children, I have been just as subject to the lies of the enemy as is typical in the Church today. We are all a part of our up-bringing and the exposures we received during that time. This includes the teaching we received in the Public Schools and our Religious Training. By the grace of God, the Bible was the first school book utilized in the Public School. This blessing permeated the whole public school system at that time. One Book, such as the Ma'Guffey Reader, which had many wonderful stories with a biblical theme, was one of the first text books used in the Schools in this country.

From the 1880's to the early 1960's, America was under the influence of a Christian heritage in the public schools. After the first three years of the 1970's, laws, policies, practices and programs began to change. Child abuse laws began to pop-up, taking authority from parents and putting fear in parents that the law would come after them if the parents spanked their own children. Policies in the public schools also reflected through the Education Code, a State centered authority over the home. In addition, practices in the schools reflected what is referred to as 'Political Correctness'. This meant that all things are given the same value. The program was generally referred to as 'VALUES CLARIFICATION' Right and wrong took on the same 'Relative

Value'. The final nail in the coffin of Christian influence in the Public School System was the rejection of the Phonics based Reading Programs used before 1973 in most of the State School Systems.

During this same time period, Science took on the same relative value as Religion as an authority. The Space Program emerged and took on a religious—quest priority. For the past (50) fifty years, we as a Nation have been subject to these new norms and the generation that went through them don't know the old God centered norms. You can see the problem. 'The people perish where there is a lack of knowledge'

CHAPTER 7

REFLECTIONS

In keeping with my experience, healing is a natural part of what God has built in to the human condition. Sin and all of the connected results are the problem. If we can believe the Bible, we must know that no matter what we say or act like, we can never erase the ever present Sin conscience God has put in us. This conscience is a constant reminder that we can never be good enough to meet Gods' standard. When we take Sin awareness out of our Schools, Our Public Institutions and our lives, we run the risk of self destruction with—out the knowledge of why. Children must be taught that Sin awareness is essential to Spiritual growth. With—out it, we condemn the following generations to wondering in the darkness of self—deception. That self deception says, WE CAN MAKE IT ON OUR OWN. WE DON'T NEED GOD. What could be further from the truth? Only one thing is worse and that is THINKING THAT WE ARE GOD. Both of these positions lead us to an inescapable conclusion and that is what—ever the consequence of our decisions, WE OWN IT. As a young boy growing up in Berkeley, California, I was exposed to the best and the worst of the WORLD SYSTEM. The best, because Berkeley was a community of communities and every part of the United States was some—how involved in the mix of people. This was made possible because of the one main factor that Berkeley only had one High School. In addition, The University of California was located just a few blocks up on Bancroft Street and the atmosphere was always charged with University talk. Later, many of my classmates had parents who worked at the University or were part the University Community. One such notable was Mary Lawrence, daughter of 'the O.E. Lawrence of 'Lawrence Livermore Labs.' In my senior year at Berkeley High, Mary and I were on the Student Board of Control under Mr.

Nelson. In addition, Mary was the Head Cheer-Leader for all the Football and Basketball games. Through these associations, I got to know her family and was invited to spend a few days at the family Balboa Island Summer Home after I ran in the 1956 Olympic Summer trials in the L.A. Coliseum.

As I look back with such a rich association of people and opportunities, Berkeley was ideal for me to observe people from all walks of life, and make life—long friendships which in total still last to this very day. Another opportunity from my associations with the Teaching and Coaching staff at the High School came through Coach Erikson, 'B' Basketball Coach. In my senior year Coach Erikson asked me to work with him for the summer planting tulips around 100 yard man made trout stream in Orinda, California on the top of a hill. I agreed and we worked all of two (2) months finishing the job. At the end of the job, Mr. Erikson took me down to some property he owned in Orinda on the Main Street. He told me that the owner had six (6) acres for sale right next to property that He owned and the owner was selling it for $1,200. Well Mr. Erickson reasoned that we both made $600 we could go in together and get the whole 6 acres. Long story short, I decided that I would use the $600 to go to College and invest later. Was it a good decision? Who would have known then how surrounding Towns would grow, and property values would sky-rocket up. Maybe I would have been set for life, but I value my heard earned education much more each day.

On the other hand as Berkeley grew and experienced the Turbulent 60's and 70's separation began to grow into divisions. Every—one had to have their own little piece of the Cultural Pie. The School District reacted by giving every—one a separate ethnic School identity through 'free' Federal Grant money. To a lesser degree, this is still the model minus the Federal Grant money.

Never the less I am still involved in the support of the Berkeley high School student athlete programs. In year 2006-07, I was inducted into the Berkeley High Hall of Fame, Class of 1956 for Track and Field/Basketball. This brings me to the next meaningful long term relationship with Rich Hacker/ Track Coach 1952-1967. Coach, if you knew him well, Coach Hacker if you didn't. At any rate, my first in-counter with Coach Hacker was as a 9th Grader, when BHS was grade 10 thru 12. On occasion, the 9th grade student from the three Junior High Schools would go to the High School to see who the competition was in the various events, especially if you intended on making the team as a 10th grader.

As the Lord would have it, on the day I went to the High School, Coach Hacker was having general work-outs for the sprinters and interval training for the 440. Well I had heard that you could challenge any one on the team and if you could beat them you could take their spot or run that event. I took the opportunity to challenge the top 440 runner on the team, coach Hacker said Lefty could run in his 1/2spike track shoes but I had to run in my tennis shoe. Tennis shoe had little or no traction but track shoes did. I was at a decided disadvantage that day. But as the Lord would have it, I *won the race* that day. Now the deal was sealed as far as I was concerned, but not with Coach Hacker. As soon as Coach Hacker saw the reaction after lefty got beat by a freshman and not yet at the High School, He took his track shoes off, tied the shoe strings together and threw them in the bleachers and stomped of the field.

Coach Hacker took off after Lefty and walked him into the Gym and had a heart to heart with him. When Coach Hacker came out, He made a B-line straight to me and said that he could not afford to have Lefty drop-out his senior year and I would be given a varsity spot in the 880 which I did not like to run. Gary Wood was the premier 880 yard runner for BHS at that time and I did not want to upset the apple cart again by casting my shadow over that event. I always managed to come in second, just to get the points.

In my second year, I ran the 220, 440, 880 and the 880 Relay with an eye toward preparation for the State Meet in Los Angeles at the Coliseum. We competed in the 880 Relay and it was invaluable experience. Coach Hacker had something in mind. In my senior year, 1956, everything was planned to the last detail, typical of Coach Hacker. We sat down and planned every race to the 10th of a second. Kick-off race was Hayward High School—Goal—break BHS 440 Record (50.6). Results: 49.7 new BHS Record. From then on it was off to the races every week with a new BHS school record. Result: 49.5, 49.2, 48.8, 48,7, 48.6,48.4, 48.3—North Coast Section meet 48.2 Final 48.6 State Meet Final 47.5 (Second in the Nation) To this day I remain 4th in the Nation in the 440 yard run for all time.

I recount these details about Track and Field and Coach Rich Hacker and Coach Erikson to simply demonstrate my early exposure to 'power thinking'. Power thinking which get results, is a life—long planning model.

This carried over into my adult life is a direct reflection of my aptitudes and abilities. This same power thinking was evidence in the creation of the Ford Motor Company. Mister Henry Ford had the ability to envision an assembly line from start to finish with the ability to see each work station and the vital function it would complete. He also envisioned what each work station would need in order to complete the function. This model forces the company or the individual to think through in detail every—thing needed to complete a project or produce a product.

The ultimate Power Thinker is GOD, because HE KNOWS THE END, FROM THE beginning. In addition, HE tells us to COUNT THE COST BEFORE FOLLOWING HIM. GOD indicates in the Bible that preparation is absolutely essential for success in anything under taken in this life and so He gives us Teachers. (1st Corinthians 12)

And so, my journey to divine healing began early in life. Getting to know that God was real was the starting point for me. Since I had decided that Jesus Christ was perfect as the only sure example for living and life, I started looking for men who resembled His example. Officer Paul Herrick of the Berkeley Police Department was one such man. Officer Paul Herrick was in charge of the Berkeley Junior Traffic Patrol and most of the athletes and student leadership went through this program. This officer had the very presence of firmness, fairness, self-discipline and trust. He was a marvelous example for the Berkeley youth. It became quite clear to me that by the above examples of the men I came in contact with and the example they gave to me was an indelible imprint on my life. I make this statement as a witness to the effect that a strong community value system has on young minds and the lasting influence it has on those who are a part of it.

FAMILY INFLUENCE

The corner stone to society is the family. Without this cornerstone, there is no foundation for stability for anything to rest upon. This I will now explore.

Jesus was a member of a family. Jesus was born into the world as any other person. The only question is who was his father? Jesus was the first born of Mary his mother. After Jesus was born, Mary had other children. Jesus grew up with brothers and sisters, (James, Jude, Jose and at least two sisters). The Bible says that Jesus grew up in grace in the sight of God and man. This would indicate that Jesus was subject to all of the laws and regulations of his times and met all of the requirements. The Bible states that Jesus kept all the Law. This means that Jesus kept all the Feast Days, every Sabbath and Temple observances.

I also was a member of a family. I was not the first born however. I was second in the order after my brother, Armstead Jr. Following me were my two sisters Joan and Patricia. I always thought it a little strange that we all seemed to have old English names. (Armstead Jr. Henry Edward, Joan Mary, Patricia Anne). My fathers' name was Armstead Dillard Dorsey and my Mothers' name was Mary Jane (Evens) Dorsey. The Dorsey Children also grew up in grace in the sight of man and God. The primary goal of my mother was that all of her children would not grow up as heathen, but would all be saved. That meant that we (children) would have to get up early on Sunday morning (after our Saturday night bath) and walk from 8th and Bancroft to King and Alcatraz Street where Progressive Baptist Church was located. Rain or shine, we took that three mile walk every Sunday for years and until we began earning Bus fare money. Those early years were learning years. Reading the Bible under the covers at night after lights out with a flash—light were indeed intense study sessions. You never knew when the battery would go out so you had to get it while the light was good. I will never forget those times with my brother and the word of God. We did not understand it all but it was a sure foundation.

As Jesus grew up, he began to recognize his place in the world with this statement, speaking to his mother, Mary, 'Don't you know that I must be about my fathers' business'. Jesus says this to his parents after he stays in Jerusalem after a High Holy-day, and they after three days had to return to Jerusalem looking for him. The Bible states that Jesus was then 12 years old. According to Jewish tradition the child becomes accountable to God at the age of 12.

The Dorsey family also recognized the same accountability for responsibility to God at the age of 12. We called it a public testimony or witness in front of the Church. Some Churches call it Confirmation. You could not just sit in your seat and meditate quietly in your place and THINK your salvation into being. You HAD TO SPEAK OUT LOUD IN FRONT OF THE WHOLE CONGRGATION WHY YOU WERE RECIVING JESUS AS YOUR LORD AND SAVIOR. It was no different with me. The lead up to my decision was interesting. The Church had obtained a copy of a movie called 'KING OF KINGS' by Cecil B. De-Mill. It was a silent movie with caption beneath to read. As I watched the movie on that Saturday night and read the captions of the movie, **THE LORD BEGAN TO SPEAK TO MY HEART.** This is for you, and, I began crying in the inner recesses of my heart. As the movie concluded, with the final scene, Jesus was just about to die and he said 'It is finished'. It was then that I understood that I did not have to carry any more guilt around with me for my sins. Jesus paid it for me, and 'It is finished'. Now I had a dilemma. Up until then, I had not made a public declaration of my faith in Jesus Christ. I was 12 years old and it was accountability time. The next day on Sunday, Sure enough the Pastor gave the invitation to come forth after his sermon. He also referred to the 'King of Kings' movie. That was the final nail in the coffin. I knew he was talking to me.

My initial reaction was fear. I did not want to get up in front of over 200 or 300 people and give my testimony, it was quite intimidating. Needless to say I did not go. Especially since no one else came forward either. However, I made myself a promise that day after service when my courage came back. I said to the Lord, I will do it next week if you let me live, I will serve you. Long story short, that week went by so quickly, it seemed I was floating on clouds the whole week in anticipation. Sunday came and the invitation to come forward was given, I was the first one to respond. Tears and crying, relief and joy all at the same time, Pastor Stovall was so patient with me I must have cried a t least two minutes. Finally, the question came. Why did you come up here to give your life to Jesus Henry? Well the answer came out of nowhere, 'if Jesus could die for me, I can live for him'. Well, that was the beginning point of many wonderful experiences living that out.

And by the way 15 or more other people got up, came forth, and gave their lives to Jesus that Sunday, evidently, every—one was waiting on me. Isn't that just like the Holy Spirit.

Not much is spoken of Jesus between his 12th and 30th birthday. It would appear that Jesus, being the eldest Son of Mary had assumed the responsibility for his mother because Joseph is not mentioned in the life of Mary or Jesus in the Gospels except in hindsight. However, Jesus was well known because of his practice of going to to the temple daily and was with the scribes and doctors of the Law. In fact, Jesus often taught them the things that they should have already known. So when Jesus said 'you hypocrites and blind guides 'speaking to the ones who were leading the people, he was speaking from experience with them, whom he knew well. Even members of Jesus own family had some issues with the way Jesus acted at times, especially when he taught out—side of the traditions. On an occasion when Jesus was in a house teaching and healing, his mother and sisters were out—side and sent for Jesus to come out because they thought he was (crazy) beside himself.

In my family I see some parallels to the experiences Jesus also went through. Families can and do put strong pressures for you to conform to group norms within the family. However, if the family norm is out—side of the written will of God, then the norm should be discarded. In my family norm, healing was not the norm. My family norm was to work it out first by natural means then turn it over to the Doctors. Jesus would only heal if asked but you had to put your—self at his complete mercy. So when I introduced my—self to the family as some—one God had revealed many healing ways to, it was like them responding to the weather 'Oh, that's nice,' like they never even heard you, or be careful of that kind of thinking, that's what *the cult people teach* (you fill in the blank). I have learned to be thick skinned when it comes to teaching the word of God because it will not always be received in the way it should be to do the most good in a person's life. The challenge for the *teacher* is to make *clear* what God has *made known.* The challenge for the *student* is to *search out a thing* so that they may *under-stand* what God has *made known.* This is a life—long endeavor. How diligent you are will determine your success. Always be prepared to give an answer to them *who want to know* the reason for the hope that lay with-in you.

The last comparison to the life of Jesus for this illustration is that Jesus never pursued people it was his words that drew people to him. It was said of Jesus that he went about teaching the people, healing them and doing good. Often Jesus would speak to the common man in easy to understand language but speak to the religious leaders in parables. As I examined this I discovered that Jesus did not want the religious leaders to *understand.* The reason is that it was already fore-told in the Scriptures that, hearing, they would hear and not understand and that seeing they would see not perceive what they were directed to look at. (Isaiah)

Jesus sums it up in Matthews 5: 1-20. 'And seeing the multitude, he went up into a mountain: and when he was set, his disciples came to him: v2. And he opened his mouth, and taught them, saying, v3.*Blessed are the poor in spirit: for theirs is the kingdom of heaven. v4. Blessed are those that mourn: for they shall be comforted. v5. Blessed are the meek: for they shall inherit the earth. v6. Blessed are they which do hunger and thirst after righteousness: for they shall be filled. v7. Blessed are the merciful: for they shall obtain mercy. v8. Blessed are the pure at heart: for they shall see God .v9. Blessed are the peacemakers: for they shall be called children of God. v10. Blessed are those who are persecuted for righteousness sake: for theirs is the kingdom of heaven. v11. Blessed are you, when men shall revile you, and persecute you, and say all manner of evil against you falsely, for my sake. v12. Rejoice and be exceeding glad: for great is your reward in heaven: for so they persecuted the prophets which were before you.* Now Jesus makes a shift, **v13. You are the salt of the earth: but if the salt have lost *its flavor,* wherewith shall it be salted? It is thenceforth good for nothing, but to be cast out, and be trodden under foot of man. (Jesus makes it clear that the flavor of salt must give a certain taste, if it does not, it is useless.) (In addition 'lost his flavor' point to our personal testimony of what Jesus has done for us, as we follow and testify of Him.**

Jesus gives us a guide and blue print of behavior and expectations when we are blessed to be in the Kingdom of Heaven. v14. *You are the light of the world. A city that is set on a hill cannot be hid. v15. Neither do men light a candle, and put it under a bushel, but on a candlestick; and it give light unto all that is in the house. v16. Let your light so shine before men, that they may see your good works, and glorify your Father which is in heaven. v17. Think not that I am come to destroy the Law, or the Prophets: I am not come to destroy, but to fulfill. v18. For verily I say unto you, Till heaven and earth pass, one jot or one title shall in no way pass from the law, till all be fulfilled. v19. Whosoever therefore shall break one of these least commandments, and shall teach men also, he shall be called least in the kingdom of heaven: but whosoever shall do and teach them, the same shall be called great in the kingdom of heaven. v20. For I say unto you, that except your righteousness shall exceed the righteousness of the Scribes and the Pharisees, you shall not enter into the kingdom of heaven.* **(The Scribes and the Pharisees were great at speaking the Law but not doing the Law). So our righteousness must exceed the righteousness of the Scribes and the Pharisees by doing the Law. (Putting into practice what the Law says). It is a natural expectation that once a person makes a declarative statement about anything, the next logical expectation is a demonstration of proof. I firmly believe that Jesus taught in the Synagogue daily, (just as the bible indicates) and afterwards went out among the people and demonstrated His teaching by healing the people. This seemed to infuriate the Scribes and the Pharisees because Jesus could back up His teaching with absolute proof of the truth of His words. And if you notice from the New Testament account, the Scribes and the Pharisees followed Jesus around watching Him to catch Him in an error. When they could not, They began to worry that the people would**

look exclusively to Jesus for all of their Spiritual needs. This is exactly what happened, even to the point that the people wanted to make Jesus their King. It was the loss of AUTHORITY among the people that made the Scribes and Pharisees want to kill Jesus. And so it is the sane with us today, not everyone will be happy with your success.

CHAPTER 8

Press On Anyway

Finish what you started, Press on, don't give up and you will get results. My personal experience came in the form of personal experience with sickness in my own body. I stopped saying things like 'I feel sick ', 'I think I am getting a cold', 'I feel like I am getting the flu'. I began to notice that if I did not give power to the thought by speaking it, I would not get the symptoms or the illness. This led me to be really careful about what I said in everything pertaining to LIFE. I started to examine my words very carefully before I spoke. I also noticed that people began paying close attention to what I said. My family began to challenge some of my words when they started hearing my words of healing. And when they did not hear me say, as follow up, 'if it be Gods' will' (This was their escape clause). That what, I was saying, if it did not come to pass, then it must not have been Gods' will that I did not get what I asserted with my words. The funny part about this is I would quote directly from the Scripture and the next word out of their mouth was, 'that was for the Apostles and not for today' (Another escape clause). What I meant buy the term (escape clause) is that, who-ever offers up an excuse for why they are not doing what Jesus said to do is that they MAY have been indoctrinated with Faulty teaching or because they are NOT DOING the WORK that JESUS said to do. I became convinced that I was on the right track and began to search the Scripture for more proof of TRUTH. As I stated earlier, The Book of Matthew was a Key to many of the examples God began to show me.

I began to listen to Preachers and Teachers on the Radio and Television. I began to compare what I was being taught By the Spirit of God to the words that they were speaking and their doctrine. What were they saying, were they doing what they were teaching or were they just repeating platitudes and traditions. I discovered that much of what was being taught AS TRUTH was from the persons' Denominational teaching and Traditions of belief, some good and bad.

I began to wonder, what scriptural foundation in the Bible that could confirm what I was observing. The first thing that the Holy Spirit revealed to me was the Book of Revelation, (the Book most every—one is fearful of and very few attempt to teach.) I noticed that Revelation 1:11 lays it all out when Jesus names the seven Churches. They are Ephesus, Smyrna, Pergamos, Thyatira, Sardis, Philadelphia, and Laodicea. In the same Chapter, v.20 reveals the mystery of seven Churches that are both historical and literal. Jesus, Jesus reveals that each Church has an Angel assigned to IT and that each Church is represented by a Candlestick. He then goes on in Chapter 2:v.1 to describe the function of each Church and the current strength and weakness. (what they are doing well and what they need to strengthen.)

It became Crystal-Clear, that one group of people (the Church) was not intended to carry the entire responsibility for the spreading of the gospel to the world. I don't believe it is coincidental that there are SEVEN CHURCHES and SEVEN CONTENENTS. God knows the hearts condition of Man and that more than one approach is needed to reach Man. I believe this is the appeal of the various denominations in the Churches today. The sad part is that the churches have segmented themselves by denominations that we no longer see ourselves as a single unified body of believers with one mission, to lift up the Name of Jesus. As pride entered into different Denominations, the view emerged that, 'One has a better approach than the other.' However, According to Revelation 2:29 Jesus says, "He that has an ear, let Him hear what The SPIRIT says unto the Churches. This is a warning that The Spirit of all Seven Churches is speaking to the one Church of JESUS CHRIST. This warning that says, 'Loss is coming if we don't pay attention to *our calling* and heed these warnings.

Jesus said in the gospels, 'the fields are ripe for the harvest, send you therefore workers into these fields'. We know that Jesus was talking about 'the world as the field and the workers as Christ followers.' Jesus is talking to all Christians, not just the Pastors or hired ministers in the Churches.

The truth is, we are all called to spread the Gospel and be ready to give a reason for the hope that lies within us. This is a part of the Great Commission, Go into all the World and preach the Gospel and these signs will follow you. You shall cast out demons, make the blind to see, make the deaf to hear, make the lame to walk, raise the dead and cure all manner of diseases. The really sad truth is that most Jesus' followers do not believe that is their calling. My observation is that Christians have been indoctrinated in the lies of Satan through traditional Denominationalism that they don't know the power GOD has invested in them by the death, burial and resurrection of Jesus Christ, that they have been lulled into sleep. In these days however, there is something stirring in the hearts of many of Gods' people which is a very good sign. There is a hunger for the truth in some of Gods' people. I see this mainly in the young people. This is not to say that older people in the church body are not tuned—into what the Spirit of God is doing. I count myself among them. But it seems to be more difficult to break the strong—hold of denominationalism from off of the older generations.

The Comfortable Illusion

When people do things over a period of time, they get comfortable. People can get comfortable with most anything. Slavery for instance as an Institution can become comfortable. The people of Moses in Egypt, became comfortable with Slavery to the point when faced with freedom and the unknown, they wanted to return to Egypt and their familiar surroundings of slavery, the food, the certainty of their old way of living. Likewise in the American Slave System, many Slaves remained on the Plantation simply because they did not know what their world would be like in a hostile unknown place. In both examples, it was the older generation that did not want to move forward with the usual objections to what lay ahead. I do not wish to minimize the real dangers that they faced but it does take courage and vision to move into unknown and uncharted waters. Jesus calls us to boldness and courage. Often, we must leave behind our comfort zone and venture in to new uncharted waters to fulfill the calling He has called us to. We have been slaves to our old-selves far too long.

It's Time to Move out

Traditions have their place, but they are not to take the place of Truth. This is the realization I had to come to when faced with doing the Word of God, instead of just knowing the Word of God. You will not move out and do the work God has for us to do unless you first trust what God has said is true. I am no different than you. I had to face this fact squarely, and Trust

Gods' Word at face value. I did not let traditional sayings or excuses get in my way, even though the thoughts kept popping up in my mind to bring doubt, I began Speaking over them. The reason I began speaking over them is, I remembered what Jesus said, 'You shall have what—ever you say.' I took this as literal then and I take this as literal today. When I say I took as literal the things I said, I spoke the out loud so I could literally *hear the words I spoke out loud with my own ears.* I did not just think words in my mind, as many of us are trained to do in our Churches. *When I spoke the words out loud I got results every—time.* Needless to say, I was excited and encouraged from then, to the present time. I came in to the *Truth Knowledge* that *God is the same yesterday, today and forever and His Word never changes or fails.* This truth put me on notice to choose my words carefully, and do not simply make idle—talk as a light thing or non effectual thing. God says that 'we shall give account for every word we say' (speak). *GOD DID NOT SAY 'we shall give account for every word we (think).*

Application

Speak to yourself first. Confirm in yourself the promises of God. You will not be confident in what you speak to others unless you know for sure that God has worked in your life the things He has confirmed in YOU. I know for a fact that God heals us through your own words. (God calls it your Faith) The very Words you speak reveals your faith. I speak to my—self on a daily basis. I speak what the Word says about my health, I speak about the Kingdom I belong to, I speak about what the king has promised to those who love Him and what He is preparing for us. I am very SPACIFIC and carful about all these things I *say.*

After gaining a victory over my own body and illnesses, I could now turn to others with a sure knowledge that God is not a respecter of persons and will do for other what he did for me.

GOD SET THE RULLS—WE LIVE BY THEM

Here are the RULES.

ASK   (SPEAK) AND IT *SHALL BE GIVEN UNTO YOU*

SEEK   (STUDY) THE WORD SO THAT *YOU KNOW WHAT TO ASK FOR*

KNOCK (EXPECT) AN *ANSWER* AND *LOOK FOR RESULTS* / GOD CAN NOT FAIL

The Holy Spirit revealed to me that WHAT GOD SPEAKS, HAS ALREADY BEEN ESTABLISHED. FROM THE INSTANT HIS SOUND GOES FORTH, IT IS ALREADY DONE. THEREFORE, WHEN WE SPEAK THE SAME WORDS THAT GOD GIVES US TO SPEAK, WE INTER INTO THE SAME REALM OF THE SAME RESULTS. IT IS ESTABLISHED, RESTING ON THE SAME FOUNDATION THAT GOD HAS ALREADY ESTABLISHED. This is marvelous to behold. I know the marvelous wonder of it all, because every time I do it, I am in awe of it. Praises be to God, I can do it and you can too. God is not concerned about our approval or disapproval of HIS RULES. He simply puts them in place for our good. We can accept them or reject them, run from them or run to them, it is our choice. WHAT EVER YOUR DECISION, THERE ARE CONSEQUENCES FOR OUR DECISIONS, POSITIVE OR NEGATIVE. His rules don't change. We are WISE if we consider this fact.

Once I learned TO SPEAK *OVER* THE PHYSICAL SICKNESS, ILLNESS AND DISEASE AND GIVE DIRECTIONS TO THEM, I LEARNED TO *SPEAK DIRECTLY TO THE SICKNESS, ILLNESS OR DISEASE, AND SEND THEM BACK TO THEIR ORIGIN, THE PIT IN THE CORE OF THE EARTH.* (Let me explain) Everything on the Earth, above the Earth or in the Earth has a name. God originally gave MAN the only AUTHORITY ON THE EARTH WHEN HE SET EVERYTHING IN PERFECT ORDER AT CREATION. (AFTER LUCIFERS' TRANSGRESION OF REBELLION IN HEAVEN)

GOD BRINGS MANKIND INTO BEING AS A DIRECT OBJECT OF JUDGEMENT AGAINST LUCIFER AND THE ANGELS THAT FOLLOWED HIM.

Now in the Genesis 1:26 account, GOD has given mankind dominion (authority) over everything that moves in the water, in the air or walks on the Earth. GOD also brought every living creature to ADAM TO SEE WHAT HE WOULD CALL THEM. (Genesis 2:19) This is the proof that GOD keeps covenant with what HE ESTABLISHES BY HIS WORDS. 'and whatsoever ADAM CALLED EVERY LIVING CREATURE, THAT WAS THE NAME THEREOF'. ADAM (man) HAS DOMINION.

Lucifer's deception in the Garden of Eden gets control of dominion over the Earth. Adam loses his dominion heritage of authority over the Earth until

JESUS OF NAZARETH GOES TO THE CROSS AND GETES IT BACK. We know this by Jesus' own words after he was Resurrected from the Dead and HE COMPLETED THE LEGAL TRANSACTION OF FULFILLING THE REQUIREMENT OF THE BLOOD COVENENT, WHERE BLOOD IS REQUIRED TO *COVER ALL SIN*. To confirm this, we read JESUS own words in Matthew 28:18, '*ALL POWER IS GIVEN UNTO ME IN HEAVEN AND EARTH*. Vs.19'GO YOU THEREFORE, AND TEACH ALL NATIONS, BAPTISING THEM IN THE NAME OF THE FATHER, AND OF THE SON, AND OF THE HOLY GHOST; vs20'TEACHING THEM TO OBSERVE ALL THINGS WHATSOEVER I HAVE COMMANDED YOU; AND, LO, I AM WITH YOU ALWAYS, EVEN TO THE END OF THE (AGE) WORLD. *AMEN.*

NOW, SINCE OUR AUTHORITY HAS BEEN RESTORED, WE CAN EXERSISE THE ORIGINAL DOMINION OVER THE THINGS OF EARTH. THIS ENCLUDES ALL OF THE SICKNESSES, ILLNESSES AND DISEASES THAT SIN BROUGHT INTO THE WORLD. We learn to do this on an individual PERSONAL basis first. We then learn to apply it to others WHEN THEY ASK FOR IT. JESUS DID THIS ALL THE TIME. In the case of blind Bartameus, who was sitting by the side of the road as he HEARD that JESUS was passing by. He yells out, 'JESUS, thy Son of David have mercy on me'. JESUS KEEPS WALKING. Bartameus yells even louder, JESUS, THY SON OF DAVID have mercy on me. JESUS stops, and says, bring THAT MAN HERE.

At this point, we must stop and ask ourselves some questions.(1) Did not Jesus hear the man when he first cried out? (2) Why did Jesus keep on walking after he heard him cry out the first time? (3) Why did Jesus stop after he heard the man cry out the second time? (4) Why did Jesus tell those who were with him to bring the man over to him? (5) Why did Jesus ask the man what did he want? (6)Did Jesus not know that the man was blind? (7) Once the man is in-front of Jesus, and Jesus sees that the man was blind. WHY ON EARTH DID JESUS ASK THE MAN WHAT DID HE WANT? (8) Could not Jesus just simply restore the man's sight and continue on his way.

I will answer the (1-8) questions in this comprehensive summery. Jesus was always teaching the People before he went out among the people healing. On this occasion, I believe Jesus was waiting for a prime teachable moment, when everyone was paying attention to what his response would be to the blind man. Jesus sends his disciples to help the blind man over to him, because he

KNEW THE MAN WAS BLIND. The blind man had to exercise HIS FAITH BY GOING WITH THE DISCIPLES TO JESUS. Now, THE STAGE IS SET. NOW THE QUESTION COMES. *WHAT DO YOU WANT?* THE BLIND MAN responds THAT I MIGHT RECEIVE MY SIGHT. NOW the teachable moment COMES. Jesus says, BE IT UNTO YOU, *YOUR FAITH HAS MADE YOU WHOLE.* NOW AS THE CROWD HEARD THESE WORDS OF JESUS AND SAW THAT THE MAN COULD SEE, THEY COULD SEE *FAITH IN ACTION* AND *WHAT FAITH REQUIRED.*

FIRST—*ASK—JESUS*, THY SON OF DAVID *HAVE MERCY ON ME.*

SECOND—*SEEK—JESUS* WITH PERSISTENCE *DON'T WORRY ABOUT THE WHAT* OTHERS THINK,THE CROWD TOLD THE BLIND MAN TO BE SILENT, IF HE HAD, HE WOULD NOT HAVE RECEIVED SIGHT.

THIRD—*KNOCK—JESUS* WILL ANSWER OUR CALL TO BRING US TO HIMSELF EVERY TIME.

My journey to Divine Healing has taken many twists and turns through-out my 73 years. However, during all this time, I have felt that God was preparing me for something greater than just this life. To me, this meant that whatever I was being prepared for had something to do with Gods plan after this life and into eternity. To me, this life is the all encompassing school of God, which is getting people ready for the real intended purposes of eternity. How well we do will determine what assignment we will get in His Eternal Kingdom. This has been a tremendous help to me during some tough times, especially where family is concerned. We all want our family to be supportive in our endeavors, but, especially in our Spiritual development and Journey. During these times, I remember what Jesus went through with his family and neighbors and my small problems fade in comparison. In everything I have learned to look to Jesus and his example to bring me through.

(Isaiah 53:1-12 Says). Jesus grew up in a place that was dry and without nourishment spiritually. A place you would not expect to find someone sent from God. Who would believe it? He grew up not looking like anything special that we would be attracted too. He was despised and rejected of men. He was a man of sorrows and grief. Jesus was designed by God to carry sorrow and grief for us. He was smitten, afflicted, wounded, and bruised for our iniquities: the chastisement of our peace was upon him, and with his stripes *WE ARE HEALED.* We all have gone our own way, and the Lord laid it all on

Jesus. When Jesus went through it all, he did not open his mouth to complain. He was like a sheep lead out before his shearers as they afflicted him. He was crucified on a cross between two wicked men and made his grave in a rich man's place. With all this, God was pleased, because Jesus was victorious over Gods enemy and God will reward His Son along with other sons who travel the same road as did Jesus to victory. It is all because Of JESUS many will follow and be victorious.

I count myself in the People of God and the work of God. I look to Jesus the author and finisher of my faith and trust in Jesus alone because he is trustworthy.

CHAPTER 9

SUMMARY

JESUS encountered a man who came to him and said, If you are willing lord, you can heal me? JESUS SAID,' I AM WILLING', AND HEALED THE MAN.

This is the Jesus I know. He is always willing and always available. If you make the effort to come to Him, He will ALWAYS MEET YOUR NEED.

JESUS is not a respecter of persons. He is the same yesterday, today and tomorrow.

This is the Jesus that upholds me, because his word never fails. Jesus said 'you shall have whatever you say. I have discovered that Jesus has returned to us our identity with him to speak life.

JESUS said many times, 'your faith has made you whole' speaking to people who came to him. Jesus then gave them an instruction to do something or stop doing something in order to KEEP what they had just received.

I have been shown by the Holy Spirit, if you don't know your covenant authority in the WORD, THE ENEMY WILL COME BACK AT YOU TO STEAL, KILL, and to DESTROY what YOU have receive. He does this WITH THOUGHTS, IDEAS and SUGGESTIONS which run COUNTER TO WHAT GOD HAS DONE FOR YOU.

JESUS said, 'go all into the world and preach the Gospel to every creature and these signs shall follow you, you shall pick up serpents, no poison thing shall harm you, you shall cast out demons, you shall heal the sick.'

When I first read these words in the Gospels, I took them to be just for the clergy and not me. I have since been shown that every word written in the Bible is meant for every believer, and especially those WHO DON'T BELIEVE IT IS WRITTEN FOR THEM.

In my brief summary, I have provided a thought provoking (4) point picture of what for me is the essence of the Gospel in a nut shell.

1) JESUS always loves us. He loved us so much that he gave himself as a sacrifice on the Cross. He was WILLING to SUFFER AND DIE FOR US.

2) JESUS has provided HEALING FOR ALL OF US from times past to times present to time future.

3) JESUS HAS RETURNED TO US THE AUTHORITY WE LOST OVER OURSELVES TO SPEAK LIFE OVER OUR CIRCUMSTANCES. He has restored it to our faith.

4) JESUS has GIVEN US PURPOSE IN OUR AUTHORITY with CONFIDENCE.

MAY THE LORD OF GLORY, ADD WISDOM TO THE READER OF THIS WORK, AND THAT THIS LABOR OF LOVE BE A BLESSING TO THE BODY OF JESUS CHRIST, THE CHURCH.

IT IS MY PRAYER FOR THE READER THAT THEY WILL SEARCH THE SCRIPTURE FOR THEMSELVES AND LET THE HOLY SPIRIT REVEAL TO THEM ALL THE SAYINGS DESCRIBED AND NOTED BY ME, SPOKEN BY JESUS. MAY THE LORD, BY THE HOLY SPIRIT, ADD UNDERSTANDING AND WISDOM TO HIS WORD.

MY PEOPLE PERISH FOR LACK OF KNOWLEDGE

Practical Applications as applied in real-life Healing
Cause and Effect—The Soul that SINETH SHALL SURELY DIE
Sin = Sickness = Illness = Disease = *Death*
Sin = doing things your way in the face of Gods' laws
Sickness = the body tells you something is wrong—you don't feel right
Illness = the symtoms don't go away, they become cronic, and stay
Disease = if unchecked the disease becomes fatal resulting in death

AN EXAMPLE

You don't wear a coat when it is cold—You are sinning against your body. You get runny nose, cough, sneezing. You now have a Illness
The result—You catch get a cold—now you have a Sickness

You seek help from a Doctor—He gives you something for your symtoms—You are still not wearing your coat and it is still cold—You now have an Illness.

The Result—You go back to the Doctor—Now He tells you, you have Pneumonia—The Doctor gives you antibiotics and puts you in the hospital and gives orders to keep you warm. You now have a Disease

If not treated properly this disease will lead to death

Remedy

If you had worn a coat in the first place you would not have sinned against your body. There are physical laws that must obey if you expect to live a hazard free life in the physical world. There are also Spiritual Laws that must also be obeyed if you expect to live a hazard free life in the Spirit

Spirit Law—Helps

You must learn to speak to whatever physical condition you face, large or small. Every Sickness, Illness and Disease is under your authority as a Child of GOD. First, you must state the facts out loud and verbally.

You will say too, Sickness, Illness and Disease, (be they a family member or anyone else, name the disease) I speak to you now in the Almighty name of Jesus of Nazareth, I command you to come off of my body right now. I am a Child of GOD and you have no authority over my body. By the Authority vested in me by Jesus, I command you (cancer) to go back to the Pit Now, In JESUS MIGHTY NAME. Then say, It is done, Angels enforce my words. (immediately do something you could not do)

OTHER EFECTIVE WORDS that bring RESULTS

1) **I shall live and not die—I serve a Living GOD—JESUS is my Salvation**
2) **I am a Child of GOD—No weapon formed against me shall prosper**
3) **JESUS IS MY LORD AND SAVIOR**
4) **JESUS is my SHEPARD and it is he who GIVES ME REST FROM ALL MY CARES**

5) **JESUS IS MY PROVIDER AND HIS SUPPLY NEVER ENDS**
6) **JESUS IS MY HEALER AND REDEEMER**
7) **JESUS MY REDEEMER LIVES AND SO SHALL I**

THEREFORE, I COMMAND YOU SICKNESS, ILLNESS AND DISEASE TO BE UNDER THE AUTHORITY OF THE ONE AND ONLY POWERFUL NAME OF JESUS OF NAZARETH TO GO BACK TO THE PIT NOW. IN JESUS NAME YOU HAVE NO AUTHORITY OVER ME HERE.

***AS JESUS PROCLAIMED FROM THE CROSS ON CALVARY, 'IT IS FINISHED'* I NOW PROCLAIM IT DONE—AMEN—AMEN—AMEN**

AMEN TO THE FATHER—AMEN TO THE SON—AMEN TO THE SPIRIT

HENRY E. DORSEY

N0VEMBER 24, 2010 revised March 25, 2011

**A PATH WELL TRAVELED BY THOSE WHO HAVE GONE
BEFORE US AND MADE SAFE PASSAGE**